The Funniest People Who Live Life

David Bruce

Published by David Bruce, 2023.

While every precaution has been taken in the preparation of this book, the publisher assumes no responsibility for errors or omissions, or for damages resulting from the use of the information contained herein.

THE FUNNIEST PEOPLE WHO LIVE LIFE

First edition. January 22, 2023.

Copyright © 2023 David Bruce.

ISBN: 979-8215423332

Written by David Bruce.

Table of Contents

Cover Illustration for *The Funniest People Who Live Life*:
Copyrighted by the Artist: Carla Evans

***

Shown in Illustration:
Tiffany and Camden Evans

***

Dedicated with Love to Carla Evans and Tiffany and Camden Evans

***

This is a short, quick, and easy read.

Anecdotes are usually short humorous stories. Sometimes they are thought-provoking or informative, not amusing.

***

Educate Yourself
Read Like A Wolf Eats
Be Excellent to Each Other
Books Then, Books Now, Books Forever

***

Do you know a language other than English? If you do, I give you permission to translate this book, copyright your translation, publish or self-publish it, and keep all the royalties for yourself. (Do give me credit, of course, for the original book.)

Chapter 1: From Actors to Christmas

Actors

• In the old days, acting was looked down on as an improper and immoral profession. The 19th-century actor O. Smith once worked in a troupe that performed in a theater that had been a chapel. The troupe made arrangements to lend the theater to a Methodist preacher on Sundays — provided that the preacher would refrain from criticizing their profession. Mr. O. Smith and a scene painter worked on Sunday, with only a curtain separating them from the preacher, so that they were able to hear every word of his sermon. Every time the preacher began to criticize the acting profession, the scene painter said "Ahem" loudly, and the preacher toned down his rhetoric. Mr. Smith writes that the ahems were "a sad restraint" on the preacher's eloquence.[1]

• One of the best movies by Mel Brooks is *The Producers*, starring Zero Mostel and Gene Wilder. Mr. Mostel was hired first, and he attended Mr. Wilder's audition. Before the audition, Mr. Mostel reached out his hand as if he were going to shake Mr. Wilder's hand, then suddenly he grabbed Mr. Wilder, pulled him close, and kissed him on the lips. Before the kiss, Mr. Wilder had been nervous, but after the kiss, he relaxed. (By the way, both Mr. Mostel and Mr. Wilder are straight.)[2]

• In Los Angeles, California, an actress friend of comedian Bob Smith was going to an audition when she became involved in a serious car accident. Although she was injured and being helped by paramedics and police, she kept telling them, "I'm got to call my agent. Please, I've got to call my agent." She knew she sounded ridiculous, but she was worried that her new agent would think she was irresponsible.[3]

• Barbra Streisand is not superstitious, although she does say that it is bad luck to step in front of a speeding locomotive. Another person who is not superstitious is Noël Coward, who nevertheless admits that it is bad luck for 13 people to sleep in the same bed.[4]

Advertising

• Professional golfer Bryon Nelson once was offered $500 to endorse the cigarettes of a certain tobacco company. This was big money at the time, and Mr. Nelson accepted it. However, he had second thoughts when Sunday School teachers started writing him to ask, "How could you?" These letters upset Mr. Nelson, and he contacted the tobacco company and tried to give the money back. Unfortunately, the tobacco company refused to let him out of his contract and so the advertisements stayed in circulation.[5]

• Sometimes, advertising is true. Once, Westbrook Van Voorhees was announcing a program sponsored by a cigarette company when he suddenly had a coughing attack. He explained the coughing by saying on the air, "Guess I've been smoking too much."[6]

• TV commercials for the European jeans manufactured by Diesel sometimes addressed contemporary issues. One commercial was headlined, "How to smoke 145 cigarettes a day." In it, a talking skull asks the viewers, "Man, who needs two lungs anyway?"[7]

• In the *Los Angeles Times* once appeared this ad, reproduced in its entirety: "LAST DAY TO SEND IN YOUR DOLLAR. — Box 153." Thousands of people parted with their money in response to this ad.[8]

Alcohol

• While making a movie with Paramount Pictures, Victor Mature and Jim Backus dressed as Roman warriors. Mr. Mature had business to attend to away from the movie studio during lunchtime; wanting company, he asked if Mr. Backus would go with him. Having completed his business, Mr. Mature and his guest stopped by a bar to have a drink, but the bartender — not being used to such guests — ignored their orders and stared at them. Mr. Mature then asked, "What's the matter with you? Don't you serve members of the Armed Forces?"[9]

• Richard Westrop, a Quaker preacher, once traveled by train and got a piece of grit in his eye. He went to the refreshment room at York (England) station and ordered a glass of milk. However, when he started to drink the milk, he discovered that alcohol had been added to it. Mr. Westrop told the server about the addition, but she irately replied, "Now look here, when a parson comes in and orders milk and gives me a wink, what else is he ordering but what I've given you?"[10]

• Jack Norton got laughs for decades in walk-on roles in which he played a drunk. Once, a director criticized him for playing a severely drunk man. According to the director, no man could be that drunk and still stay on his feet. But the director didn't know that Mr. Norton had watched him at a party a couple of days earlier and was imitating him.[11]

• Bishop Healy of Galway once went to a barber who had been out drinking the night before. Because of the unsteadiness of his hands, the barber accidentally cut Bishop Healy, who said, "This cursed drinking!" The barber replied, "Yes — it leaves the skin awful tender."[12]

Arguments

• A Rabbi and a soapmaker were talking. The soapmaker asked, "What good is religion? After millennia of sermons and prayers, still many people lack spirituality. If religion is true, why is this so?" The Rabbi pointed to a child playing in a mud puddle and said, "Look at that child. After millennia of soapmaking, some people are still dirty. If soap makes people clean, why is this so?" The soapmaker said, "Soap cannot do any good unless it is used." The Rabbi replied, "Exactly."[13]

• Rabbi Joshua ben Hanania went to Athens to talk with some philosophers, who asked him, "Where is the center of the Earth?" Rabbi Joshua pointed to a nearby spot and said, "This is the center of the Earth." When the Athenian philosophers asked how he knew that, Rabbi Joshua replied, "Bring your measuring rods, and measure it for yourselves."[14]

• Comic singer Anna Russell's Auntie Wavell enjoyed arguing with the vicar after church. He usually would end the argument by slamming the door. Once, he slammed the door — and it fell off its hinges.[15]

Baseball

• Andy Olsen was an umpire for the longest scoreless game in baseball. On May 8, 1965, in the Eastern League, teams from Elmira, New York, and Springfield, Massachusetts, battled in a game that lasted 27 innings — the first 25 of them scoreless. In the 26th inning, both teams got a run, and in the 27th inning, Elmira won the game, 2-1, with a close play at home plate. The Springfield coach wasn't happy, but he didn't argue the call. Instead, he told Mr. Olsen, "Andy, you shortened the game on us."[16]

• Francis Cardinal Spellman attended the 1953 World Series between the Brooklyn Dodgers and the New York Yankees. In one game, Dodger catcher Roy Campanella ran after a foul ball that struck a railing, then bounced off Cardinal Spellman's knee. Mr. Campanella asked whether His Eminence had been hurt. "Don't worry about me," Cardinal Spelling replied. "God had the wisdom to make a priest's knees the toughest part of his anatomy."[17]

Bathrooms

• When the Middleroad Friends Meeting in Springport, Indiana, renovated its bathrooms, it was a big deal, and the Quakers attending the meeting decided to celebrate. First, a nicely varnished plunger — the Plunge Ahead Award — was presented to the clerk. Second, the meeting's sole doctor member presented the meetinghouse with a bunch of old magazines for reading purposes. Third, brass plates — one showing a woman's bonnet and the other showing a man's broad-brimmed hat — were put on the relevant doors. Fourth, a ceremonial cutting of a roll of toilet paper was held. Fifth, two children — a boy and a girl — performed ceremonial flushes. And finally, tours of the facilities were held. Often, Quakers are thought to be overly solemn, but obviously, that stereotype is not true of the Middleroad Friends Meeting.[18]

• A Western woman went to a Zen monastery to seek enlightenment. While there, she cleaned the bathrooms in an effort to show that she was humble. In addition, she pestered the Zen master by constantly asking, "What is Zen?" The Zen master ignored her. Eventually, she got tired of cleaning the bathrooms and told the Zen master that if she wanted to clean bathrooms, she could do that anywhere and therefore she was leaving the monastery. The Zen master replied, "That is Zen."[19]

Bible

• In his absence, the Irish Republican Army once sentenced Irish playwright Brendan Behan to death. Mr. Behan sent the IRA "a polite note, saying that they could shoot me in my absence, also." And in a court of law, a man denied three times that he knew Irish playwright Brendan Behan. From the back of the court, a supporter of Behan's crowed, "Cock-a-doodle-doo."[20]

• William Schwenck Gilbert, co-author of *The Pirates of Penzance*, occasionally criticized the Church. Once he found himself the only layman in a room filled with parsons and remarked, "I feel like a lion in a den of Daniels."[21]

• For decades, Abel Green edited *Variety*, the bible of show business. Its readership was wide and varied; for example, when Mr. Green met Francis Cardinal Spellman, the Cardinal said, "Mr. Green, I read *your* bible, too."[22]

Books

• In the late 1800s, many rabbis and Jewish families regarded the reading of many books not religious in nature — for example, novels — as dangerous. Joseph Salz, who lived in Palestine, was one person who believed this, but his wife, Hannah, did not. Joseph once caught Hannah reading a novel, so he forbade her to read it. She obeyed him for a while, then she started to read novels again. The next time Joseph caught her reading a novel, he burned it. However, in the long run, Hannah won — she helped her daughters acquire a good education at a time when educated women were rare.[23]

• Pulitzer Prize-winning reporter Meyer Berger was Jewish, but he wrote well and positively about Catholic missionaries in his book *Men of Maryknoll*, which was co-written with the Reverend James Keller. Pope Pius XII once gave him an audience in which he thanked him for writing the book and then blessed him. Mr. Berger was flustered and replied, "God bless you, too, sir."[24]

• Comedian Bob Newhart is in many ways a modest man. When he heard that Jeff Sorensen was writing a biography of him, Mr. Newhart asked, "Why would anybody want to do a book about me? It would have to be about eight pages long." (Actually, the biography turned out to be about 180 pages long.)[25]

Celebrities

• Lou Costello told Jackie Gleason that he knew a man who could tell what card you were holding even though he was miles away and talking to you on the telephone. Jackie then picked the Jack of Diamonds and showed it to Lou, who made a telephone call, saying, "Hello, is the Wizard there? ... Would you put him on, please? ... Jackie Gleason would like to speak to you." Jackie then spoke to the Wizard, who told him, "You are holding the Jack of Diamonds." Of course, there was a logical explanation. Lou was calling his partner, Bud Abbott. When Lou asked for the Wizard, Bud immediately recited, "Spade ... heart ... diamonds ..." — when the right suit was named, Lou asked that the Wizard be put on the line. Bud would then recite "Ace ... King ... Queen ... Jack ..." — when the right denomination was reached, Lou said that Jackie wanted to speak to the Wizard.[26]

• Much of W.C. Fields' comic character was formed during his hard times as a youngster. He was beaten up by bullies so often that his nose grew enormously because of scar tissue. (Yes, Mr. Fields did drink, but the big nose came about because of the fights.) He acquired his raspy voice because of all the colds he got through exposure. His favorite way of warming up after a cold night was to lean with his back against a high board fence; as the sun warmed the boards, the boards warmed him. Also, the "fraudulent grandiosity" (Robert Lewis Taylor's apt phrase) that was so much a part of Mr. Fields' on-screen character came about because of the respect he received from other youngsters because he was living on his own and because of his many arrests.[27]

• Perry Como really was an easy-going celebrity. Comedy writer Goodman Ace came up with this joke for him: "I was trapped in my house all summer with my kids playing the jukebox, records, and all that. It was the summer of my discotheque!" However, Mr. Como wasn't sure that the joke was all that funny, so it was given to the show's announcer, Frank Gallop. During rehearsal, the joke got a big laugh, and Mr. Como said, "If I had known it would get that big of a laugh, I wouldn't have given it to Frank." When Mr. Goodman suggested that he take the line back, since he was the star of the show, Mr. Como was shocked: "Oh no. You can't do that."[28]

• One of the early "dumb" blonde actresses was Marie Wilson. One day, Marie was sitting in a nightclub, when the nightclub comics — all of whom were adlibbers known for making fun of anyone who came near them — came to her table and asked her to say a few words. Her date shook his head at her, warning her not to say anything because the comics would cut her to pieces, but Ms. Wilson simply said these words into the comics' microphone: "Don't drink your bathwater." This caused the nightclub comics to laugh so hard that they were incapable of saying anything.[29]

• Entrances matter in Hollywood. Actress Maria Montez would wear an Arabian Nights costume, then walk into the Sun Room, where important movie executives ate at the Universal Pictures commissary. If no important executives were in the Sun Room when she made her entrance, she would wait in the ladies room until some important executives entered the Sun Room, then make her entrance again. Lou

Costello also knew how to make an entrance; he once entered the Sun Room accompanied by a three-piece band.[30]

• Groucho Marx made fun of many kinds of pomposity. Once, he attended a séance run by the mysterious Narobi, who claimed to be able to get in touch with spirits such as that of George Washington. Once Narobi entered the spiritual world, she would allow members of the audience to ask questions of the dead. Think of it! What would you ask Homer, or Lincoln, or Napoleon? Groucho's hand shot up, and he was allowed to ask his question: "Narobi, what's the capital of North Dakota?"[31]

• Danny Thomas was Semitic, being of Lebanese origin. A Catholic, he frequently ate as a guest at the Hillcrest Country Club, whose membership was restricted — to Jews only. After the club began to admit Gentiles as members, he applied for admission but was turned down. When Mr. Thomas asked why, the management explained, "We decided that if we were going to admit Gentiles they should look like Gentiles."[32]

• Humor writer Cathy Crimmins was different even in high school. Besides being very tall, she wore evening gowns to pep rallies, she listened to albums such as *Bobby Short Sings Cole Porter*, and her three best friends were a gay man, a black man, and a Jewish man. In addition, her parents were different. For example, when someone died, her father would say, "He won't do *that* again!"[33]

• In 1997, Phyllis Diller, who was famous in part for her jokes about plastic surgery, celebrated her 80th birthday. She told her guests, "More men have worked on my face than on the Egyptian pyramids." To back up her statement, she gave each guest a list of the plastic surgery procedures she had undergone — the list included 18 improvements to her face and figure.[34]

• The Countess Anna de Noailles (1876-1933) possessed an ego that may have been a little too healthy. During a discussion about whether God exists, she said, "It's as simple as this: If God were to exist, I should be the first to be informed."[35]

Charity

• Dick Gregory grew up poor, and he was acquainted with well-intended charity that could have been handled better. At Christmas one year, a charity worker knocked on his family's door and offered him a free turkey, but he shut the door in her face — the utilities had been turned off because there was no money to pay the bills, and so there was no way to cook the turkey. Another time, he and several other children in the neighborhood received the gift of a warm jacket. However, Dick threw his jacket away because all the jackets were the same color and style, so other people could glance at his jacket and know immediately that he was a recipient of charity. As an adult, Mr. Gregory became a comedian and made people laugh.[36]

• In 1948, Jean Carroll did a benefit for the United Jewish Appeal. Her greatest applause came when she said, "I've always been proud of the Jews, but never so proud as tonight because tonight I wish I had my old nose back."[37]

• James M. Barrie, the author of *Peter Pan*, was very generous in giving to charity. He often gave away copies of his original writings to charities so that they could be auctioned off to raise money.[38]

Children

• Emperor Fo-siu respected the Buddhist priest Si-tien and told him that he could have any treasure — including gold, silver, jewels, priceless works of art — he wanted, provided that he could carry it away in one trip. He then gave Si-tien the key to the royal treasure rooms. However, Emperor Fo-siu was surprised to see Si-tien return very quickly, leading a small girl by the hand. Emperor Fo-siu told Si-tien, "I wanted to give you something valuable, not a dirty orphan. Why did you choose her?" Si-tien replied, "In choosing the child, I chose many rewards — smiles, laughter, affection, small hands and feet, ribbons thrown about in disarray, and the love of a small child for a caring parent."[39]

• Diwali, the Hindu Festival of Lights, is celebrated with good fellowship, good food, and lots of lights. Hindus turn on every light in the house, leave tiny clay lamps called dipa (DEE-pa) burning outside, and often string white electric lights around the outside of houses and turn them on. In addition, children often play "Pin the Flame on the Dipa." This is similar to "Pin the Tail on the Donkey," but the blindfolded children try to pin the picture of a flame onto a lamp.[40]

• Eddie Cantor was a fabulously successful comedian in the first half of the 20th century. His children were autograph collectors, and so one day he offered to sign his name in their autograph books — but they wailed, "No, no, please, Daddy. These are for celebrities only."[41]

Christmas

• Many parents have difficulty sleeping in on Christmas — not because they don't want to, but because their children are so eager to open presents. Olympic gymnast Shannon Miller's mother, Claudia, found a way to sleep in a little longer. She used to hide one present for each child, then write a poem giving a clue to where the presents were hidden. Only after the children had found the hidden gifts were they allowed to awaken their parents. (It's a great idea, but Claudia says it resulted in only six or seven extra minutes of sleep, as her children were wonderful at figuring out the hiding place of the presents.)[42]

• When Gary Paulsen, author of *Hatchet*, was only four years old, he visited a very ill young cousin named Raleigh. Raleigh's parents knew that their child would die soon, so they made Christmas special that year. On Christmas Eve, Santa Claus pulled up to Raleigh's house in a sleigh driven by four reindeer. Young Gary touched one of the reindeer to see if it was real. It was. He also pulled Santa's beard to see if it was real. It was. You can read more about this special, true event in Mr. Paulsen's book *A Christmas Sonata*.[43]

• One December 22, opera singer Leo Slezak received a large potted palm as a Christmas gift. Meeting the hired deliverer at the door, he immediately wrote a new card and had the plant sent to his lawyer, rejoicing that that was one gift he wouldn't have to buy. However, late on Christmas Eve the potted palm was once again delivered to his house. In the past two days, the potted palm had passed through seven different owners — each one writing a new card and sending the plant on to another person.[44]

• Before the days of air conditioning, many residents of New York City used to leave the metropolis in the summer and move to a cooler, more rural location. For that reason, humorous writer Oliver Herford used to keep his Christmas cards until July, then open them. He explained, "When other people's friends have gone away for the summer and neglect them, it certainly is gratifying and exciting to be cheerily greeted by everyone you know."[45]

• Conductor Arturo Toscanini and composer Giacomo Puccini were friends, although sometimes they feuded. During one feud, Puccini forgot to take Toscanini's name off his Christmas list, so Toscanini received a loaf of the bread known as panettone. When Puccini discovered the oversight, he wired Toscanini: "Panettone sent by mistake. Puccini." In reply, he received this telegram: "Panettone eaten by mistake. Toscanini."[46]

• Musician's Bill Worland's father was a British soldier during World War I, and he told about celebrating Christmas as a soldier during wartime. Ceasefire was called on Christmas, and enemy soldiers visited the other side's trenches, ate together, and displayed photographs of family. At midnight, the ceasefire ended, and the soldiers settled down again to the business of killing each other.[47]

• On December 16, 1965, astronauts Walter M. Schirra and Tom Stafford, after having rendezvoused with another space vehicle, called NASA to report a UFO. This UFO was strangely familiar, with eight power plants and a command module bearing a red-suited astronaut.

After reporting the UFO, Mr. Schirra and Mr. Stafford played "Jingle Bells."[48]

• Figure skating competitively can be expensive, as skates, time to practice on the ice, and coaches all cost money. When Michelle Kwan was young, her family couldn't afford to buy a Christmas tree one winter, so she entered a contest at school and won one.[49]

• At a Montreal-New York hockey game, sportscaster Frank Selky, Jr., interviewed a young boy and asked whether he had had a nice Christmas. The boy said, "No." When Mr. Selky asked why not, he replied, "I'm Jewish."[50]

• One of figure skater Tara Lipinski's favorite foods is milkshakes, and so one year her parents got her a blender for Christmas. In 1998, Ms. Lipinski won an Olympic gold medal in women's figure skating.[51]

• Jewish comedian Milton Berle once gave the president of one of his fan clubs a special Christmas gift. She was shy because she had a large nose, so Mr. Berle got her a nose job.[52]

Chapter 2: From Church to Doctors

Church

• Luigi (his name at birth was Eugene Louis Faccuito), a dancer who developed the Luigi technique that helped his own rehabilitation after a crippling automobile accident, went home for a wedding. His mother told him that he must go to Holy Communion. Luigi protested, "I can't. I didn't go to confession, and now it's too late. It's almost midnight." His mother then insisted that he go to confession before the ceremony, but Luigi again protested, "If I go to confession before the ceremony, there will be no ceremony. I haven't been to confession in 25 years." His mother replied, "All you have to say is, 'Bless me, Father, for I have sinned. I am in show business.'"[53]

• In Southampton, England, one of the shortest sermons in history was given at St. Andrew's Dune Church. The week had been extremely hot, and the entire sermon consisted of these words by guest minister Reverend William Henry Wagner: "If you think it's hot here, just wait." Reverend Linda Poindexter at Christ Episcopal Church in Rockville, Maryland, gave another short sermon. It was a hot day, and the air conditioning wasn't working. Reverend Poindexter's entire sermon consisted of these words: "Hot, isn't it? Hell's like that. Don't go there! Amen."[54]

• While in seminary, TV's Mister Rogers visited a church where he heard a sermon that he thought was terrible and violated everything that he had learned about writing and delivering sermons. However, the woman sitting next to him had tears running down her face, and she whispered, "He said exactly what I needed to hear." That day, Mister Rogers learned that "the space between a person doing his or her best to deliver a message of good news and the needy listener is holy ground."[55]

• In 1979, Russell Johnson, who played the Professor on *Gilligan's Island,* and his wife visited Westminster Abbey. Although he is normally very open to meeting fans, he disliked being mobbed in this particular place and told them, "Please, please, not in Westminster Abbey. This is a church." Once he was outside Westminster Abbey, he was again willing to pose for photographs and sign autographs.[56]

• The great dancer Bill Robinson — aka Mr. Bojangles — once went into a church, then took out a handkerchief and tied up his feet, saying, "These fools [meaning his feet] don't know they're in church. They might break out dancin' any minute. So I'm tying them up to make sure they behave!" The churchgoers loved it.[57]

• Caesar Augustus was told by the citizens of Tarraco, Spain, that an omen had occurred — a palm tree had begun to grow on his altar. Augustus was unimpressed, saying, "It is clear how often you light a sacrificial fire."[58]

• Comedian Henry Morgan traveled to France, where he saw the great cathedral at Chartres. Outside the cathedral was a sign: "NO SHORTS. NO DéCOLLETE. THIS IS A CHURCH, NOT A MUSEUM."[59]

• Peoria, Illinois, used to have a group of Ku Klux Klan believers. After it disbanded, its klavern headquarters was purchased by Mt. Zion Baptist to become the new headquarters of a black church.[60]

• Asked what work he had enjoyed the most, a Belfast demolition worker who was a Catholic replied, "Pulling down a Protestant church and getting paid for it."[61]

• As a teenager, Elvis Presley used to sneak out of his own church so he could go to a nearby black church and listen to the gospel choir.[62]

Clothing

• Charlie Erbstein, a Chicago lawyer early in the 20th century, was widely believed to be crooked. Once he was put on trial for allegedly bribing a jury, but the testimony of a priest saved him. At the exact time the jurors were being bribed, Mr. Erbstein was sitting in the priest's rectory. (The priest had taken special note of the time because Mr. Erbstein had pointed it out to him.) In gratitude for the priest's testimony, Mr. Erbstein donated a large stained-glass window to the priest's church. The window depicted a scene from the Gospels. Written on the window was the title "Christ Stripped of His Clothes," and underneath, in smaller letters, appeared "By Charles E. Erbstein." Bob Cantwell, a rival lawyer and a Catholic, once looked at the writing on the stained-glass window and said, "He's the SOB who could do it."[63]

• Children's book writer Phyllis Reynolds Naylor called her paternal grandmother "Mammaw." In rural Mississippi, Mammaw would drive her car around on Sundays picking up children to take them to church. If a child's parents objected that their child did not have clothes good enough for Sunday School, Mammaw would open the trunk of her car, rummage in a box for suitable clothing that would fit the child, dress the child, then put the child in the back seat with the rest of the church-going children.[64]

• Oliver Herford always wore suits of the same color. Mr. Herford explained that each spring he sent his tailor a sample of his dandruff and asked him to match it exactly. He once wore an outrageous derby, explaining that it was a whim of his wife's. Advised to throw the derby away, he declined, saying, "You don't know my wife — she has a whim of iron."[65]

• Monsignor Angelo Roncalli was once the Apostolic Nuncio to France, where he sometimes attended dinner parties at which women wore dresses with low necklines. At one dinner party, he offered a woman with a very low-cut dress an apple, saying, "It was only after Eve ate the apple that she became aware of how little she had on."[66]

• In Brazil, toplessness on many beaches is common. Once a Brazilian auxiliary bishop was asked his opinion of this nudity. He replied, "I am more worried about the nudity of those who have no clothes to wear."[67]

Couples

• Vanessa Alcazar wanted to attend her high school prom with that special someone — who in Vanessa's case turned out to be a girlfriend named Anna Gallegos. This upset the principal, and he told Vanessa and Anna that they couldn't attend the prom as a couple. Prominent attorney Gloria Allred called the principal, threatening to sue the school district for discrimination, and 15 minutes later the principal decided that Vanessa and Anna could attend the prom as a couple.[68]

• Katherine Hepburn was taller than Spencer Tracy. When they first met, she wore high heels to make herself even taller to intimidate him, but he declined to be intimidated. After Ms. Hepburn said, "I'm afraid I'm a little tall for you, Mr. Tracy," he replied, "Don't worry, I'll soon cut you down to my size."[69]

Dance

• Some Christians believe that dancing is a sin. American dance pioneer Ted Shawn once preached a guest sermon on a text from Psalms: "Praise ye the Lord in the dance." Mr. Shawn told the congregation, "You believe in the Bible. It is not to be interpreted allegorically. It is explicit, and you must believe in it as it is worded. Now here is a clear, curt, concise command, 'Praise ye the Lord in the dance.' Have you done so today? Then if not you have committed a sin of omission." A member of the congregation shouted, "Amen, brother!"[70]

• Helen Keller was born both deaf and blind, and it was years longer than usual before she learned to speak. Nevertheless, she was always very curious intellectually. While visiting the dance school of choreographer Martha Graham, Ms. Keller asked what jumping was. Ms. Graham had Ms. Keller place her hands on the hips of dancer Merce Cunningham, and he jumped several times. Her face radiant with joy, Ms. Keller said, "How like thought. How like the mind it is."[71]

• Sergei Diaghilev enjoyed telling this story about Vaslav Nijinsky: Mr. Nijinsky had gone to a public ball in Paris. After he and a young woman had danced together, she had told him, "You are a nice boy, but you really ought to learn to dance." Also according to Mr. Diaghilev, Mr. Nijinsky hated parties, and he had been so nervous at one party that he had chewed up his wine glass.[72]

• When American ballet master George Balanchine was asked how he managed to create his choreography, he replied, "Oh, it's really very easy. I hear music, and I see people doing things, and I just go in the studio and I have them do what I see them do in my mind." He then pointed upward and said, "He tells me."[73]

• At seven years of age, Rudolf Nureyev saw his first ballet performance. After seeing ballerina Zaituna Nazredinova dance, young Rudolf knew his life ambition. In later life, he said that he sat in the audience, watching and thinking, "I must be a dancer. I will be a dancer."[74]

• In the old days, many religious people considered dancing to be evil. When modern dance pioneer Martha Graham told her Presbyterian minister that she was going to become a dancer, he did not say anything, but simply turned his back on her and walked away.[75]

• Angelo Pietri portrayed Christ in Léonide Massine's *Laudes Evangelii*. As a result of his performance, many members of the audience came to him afterward to seek spiritual advice.[76]

Death

• When she was married to Gary Morton, Lucille Ball once visited Jackie Gleason in Florida. Mr. Gleason decided to give her the star treatment and sent a couple of off-duty police officers in a limousine to pick her and her husband up. Unfortunately, when the police officers drove up to Jackie's house and opened the door of the limousine, they found out that they had picked up the wrong Mr. and Mrs. Morton — a very scared couple from Grand Rapids, Michigan. Mr. Gleason entertained the couple and eventually an angry Lucy and her husband arrived in a taxi. By the way, shortly before Mr. Gleason died, he said, "If God wants another joke man, I'm ready."[77]

• In a Litchfield, Connecticut, cemetery is a headstone which says, "Here lies the body of Mrs. Mary, wife of Deacon John Buel, Esq. She died Nov. 4, 1768, aged 90 — having had 13 Children, 101 Grand-Children, 247 Grate-Grand-Children, and 49 Grate-Grate-Grand-Children; total 410. Three Hundred and Thirty-Six survived her." And in a Putnam, Connecticut, cemetery is a headstone that says, "Phineas H. Wright. Born in Fitzwilliam N.H. Apr. 3. 1829. Died in Putnam, Ct. May 2, 1918. Going, But Know Not Where."[78]

• The widow of a vicar was once asked about her husband's death. She replied, "I'm sure that my husband is enjoying eternal bliss. But must we talk about such an unpleasant subject?" By the way, a man named William Palmer was sentenced to death after being convicted of using poison to commit murder. As he stepped on the scaffold, he asked, "Are you sure it's safe?" Also, before he faced a firing squad, convicted criminal James W. Rodgers was asked if he had any last requests. He asked for a bulletproof vest.[79]

• Ed and Dora — a couple of distant relatives of children's mystery writer Joan Lowery Nixon — lived in Huntington Park, near Los Angeles, city of earthquakes. Ed liked to tell a story about his wife, Dora, a spiritualist preacher. Dora spent the couple of Sundays before the big earthquake of March 10, 1933, talking about how she was not afraid of death. In fact, she preached, "I welcome death." But when the big earthquake hit, Dora ran into the street and screamed at the sky, "I didn't mean it, God! I didn't mean it!"[80]

• Henry Labouchere did not take kindly to fools — even rich and powerful fools. As an assistant to an Ambassador, he once requested that a nobleman take a chair and wait to be admitted to the Ambassador. This outraged the nobleman, who protested, "Do you know who I am?" Mr. Labouchere responded, "Pray take two chairs." When Mr. Labouchere lay dying, a visitor knocked over a lamp near him. Mr. Labouchere opened his eyes, saw the fire, and then joked, "Flames? Not yet, I think."[81]

• Early in his life, Oscar Wilde flirted with becoming a Catholic. However, his half-brother Henry Wilson died, leaving Mr. Wilde £100 and a half-share in a fishing lodge — on condition that Mr. Wilde remain a Protestant for five years. On his deathbed, Mr. Wilde finally became a Catholic. As Mr. Wilde lay dying, his friend Robbie Ross brought a priest who gave him Extreme Unction after receiving him into the Church of Rome. A true wit, Mr. Wilde once said, "A poet can survive everything but a misprint" and "Bigamy is having one wife too many. Monogamy is the same."[82]

• Dorothy Parker declined to be weepy. When her husband, Alan Campbell, died, a friend stopped by and asked if he could do anything. Ms. Parker said no, but the friend insisted that there must be something he could do, so Ms. Parker said, "Well, if you insist, go to the corner and get me a tuna on rye, hold the mayo." Ms. Parker once said that she wanted her epitaph to say, "If you can read this, you're too close."[83]

• Jackie Gleason, when he weighed 280 pounds, said that he was practicing to play a golf match with Toots Shor, who weighed 275 pounds. Bob Hope said, "If those two played on the same golf course, you wouldn't see anything but shadows." When Toots Shor died, Mr. Gleason sent flowers and a card on which he scribbled, "Save a table for me, pal."[84]

• George S. Kaufman, the co-author of the play *You Can't Take It With You*, once walked into the office of eccentric Broadway producer Jed Harris, only to see that Mr. Harris was stark naked. However, Mr. Kaufman remained calm, merely remarking, "Mr. Harris, your fly is open." Mr. Kaufman once thought about putting this epitaph on his tombstone: "Over my dead body."[85]

• Phyllis Diller came up with two epitaphs for when she died: 1) "Here lies Phyllis Diller. She gave her body to Science. They didn't want it." 2) "Here lies Phyllis Diller — she looks better now than she ever has." She was cremated, and her ashes were scattered in the Pacific

Ocean. I want my own epitaph to read: "Here lies David Bruce — he finally figured out a foolproof way to lose weight."[86]

• Lauritz Melchior regarded very highly a mezuzah bearing a Star of David because it had saved his life. At an airport, he had discovered the mezuzah was missing, so he went back to his hotel to get it. His plane took off without him and crashed in the Rocky Mountains, killing everybody on board.[87]

• In a Berkshire Center, Vermont, cemetery is a headstone that bears the inscription: "When you are dressed all in your best / In fashion most complete / Think how like me you soon will be / Dressed in your winding sheet."[88]

• When the comedian W.C. Fields was ill and knew he was dying, his friend Ben Hecht saw him reading a Bible. Mr. Hecht asked, "What are you reading that book for?" A comedian to the end, Mr. Fields replied, "Looking for loopholes."[89]

• As Wilson Mizner was lying on his deathbed, a priest came into the room. Mr. Mizner looked at the priest, smiled, then said, "Father, thanks for coming but I don't need you. I'll be seeing your boss in a few minutes."[90]

• Comedian Danny Thomas' father did not go gentle into that good night. Just before he died, he sat up in bed, shook his fist toward the heavens, and shouted, "God d*mn death."[91]

• When Henry David Thoreau, author of *Walden*, was lying on his deathbed, he was asked if he had made his peace with God. He replied, "We've never quarreled."[92]

• Mark Twain once remarked that when his time came, he wanted to be cremated. His pastor replied, "I wouldn't worry about that, if I had your chances."[93]

• "I TELL YOU HERE FROM THE SHADES / IT IS ALL WORTH WHILE." — George Jessel's epitaph.[94]

Doctors

• Minor-league umpire Harry "Steamboat" Anderson had 20/20 vision — and a certificate signed by an optometrist to prove it. Whenever a player or manager questioned his eyesight, Steamboat used to show him the certificate. Steamboat also had the habit of shaking hands with veteran baseball players at the start of each season. In addition, he had the habit, after the last out of the season had been made, of turning to the fans and yelling, "God bless you," before going home.[95]

• On one of his humorous radio programs, Henry Morgan spoke about the town of More, Utah, which had only two doctors. According to Mr. Morgan, this is the place from which we get commercials saying, "More doctors recommend ...."[96]

Chapter 3: From Education to Marriage

Education

• When Garrison Keillor was in the 4th grade, Mrs. Erickson taught his class about Helen Keller, who was blind and deaf but still lived a remarkable life. She then gave the class an essay assignment: "What would you do if you had one day left to live?" Garrison knew that Mrs. Erickson wanted the class to write about such things as "smelling flowers and listening to birds sing and watching the sun set," but he wrote about what he really wanted to do, which was "to get on a plane and fly to Spain." Mrs. Erickson did have a good objection to this wish: "Spain is too far. It takes almost a day just to get there." She wanted young Garrison to pick something else to do on the final day of his life, but he declined to do that, knowing as he did — and does — that "life is the journey, not the destination."[97]

• Jean Little, the author of *Little by Little*, attended Canada's Victoria College, where the great literary critic Northrop Frye taught. While there, Ms. Little had the privilege of attending some classes taught by Professor Frye. One class was in Religious Knowledge and the English Bible. As you might expect, Professor Frye made a big impact on his students. One of the seniors at the college told Ms. Little, "In first year you believe in God. In second year you don't believe in God. In third year you believe in Frye's God. In fourth year you believe Frye is God."[98]

• Jacob Isaac was known as the *Yehudi Hakodosh* or the Holy Jew. Throughout his life, he was a scholar, arising early each day to study — a habit that he said he owed to a blacksmith. When he was young, he heard a neighboring blacksmith hammering away early in the morning, and he thought, "If my neighbor can work so hard for material things, surely I can work even harder in the service of the Lord." Each morning, the thought of the blacksmith arising early to work made him eager to begin his study.[99]

• When Francesca Gallio, age 11, interviewed TV celebrity Simon Cowell, she discovered that he actually considered himself "one of the worst-behaved people in school" when he was a kid. That is, when he actually made it to school. One of his tricks to get out of school was to put a cup of hot tea on his head for 30 seconds or so, and then say, "I'm not feeling very well, Mum. Can you feel my head?" Of course, his head would feel hot, as if he had a fever, and he got to stay home from school.[100]

• A young man came to a Zen master and asked, "How long is it going to take me to attain enlightenment?" The Zen master replied, "Ten years." The young man exclaimed, "That long!" The Zen master replied, "I have made a mistake. It will take you 20 years." The young man asked, "Why did you double the number of years it will take me to attain enlightenment?" The Zen master replied, "Now that I think about it, it will probably take you 30 years."[101]

• A man once asked Rabbi Israel Salanter for advice. He explained that he had only 15 minutes a day to devote to study, and so he asked whether he should devote that 15 minutes to studying the Torah and Talmud or to studying a *mussar* (that is, pietistic) text. Rabbi Salanter advised, "Study the *mussar* text, and it will soon make you realize that something is terribly wrong with your life if you have only 15 minutes a day to study."[102]

• Oscar Wilde was once asked to attend a dinner of the Thirteen Club — whose members disbelieved in superstition. At their dinners, members ate 13 courses while in groups of 13 people at 13 tables, then they all smashed mirrors. Mr. Wilde declined to attend the dinner, saying, "I love superstitions. ... Leave us some unreality. Do not make us too offensively sane."[103]

• Back when comedian Lea Delaria was attending Catholic schools, the nuns sometimes hit their pupils. These days, the pupil's parents would probably sue the nun, but back then when young Lea said that a nun hit her, her mother would hit her again and say, "You probably deserved it."[104]

• Yen Ho was a wise man who was asked to be the tutor to the heir of a murderous despot. Seeking advice, he went to Ch'u Po Yu and explained his situation. Ch'u Po Yu answered, "When you deal with such a person, you must first improve yourself, not him."[105]

• At Vacation Bible School, a class learned about the story of the Prodigal Son, then the teacher asked, "What does it mean to 'waste your substance on riotous living'"? A seven-year-old boy answered, "It means to spend all your money on bubble gum."[106]

• While attending Stratford High School, comedian Bill Hicks was a nonconformist. One day, a group of teenagers from a rival school drove by him and called out, "Stratford sucks." Bill replied, "Yeah, I know. I go there."[107]

Fathers

• Dionysus, the dictator of Syracuse, once criticized his son for acting inappropriately, but his son replied that Dionysus had never had a king for a father. Dionysus replied, "If you behave like that, you won't have a king for a son."[108]

• Comedian Pat Henning once toured England, then many years and a toupee later, toured England again. The toupee did its job — theater managers told him that he was much funnier than his father had been.[109]

Food

• Following the Russian Revolution of 1917, life was hard and pets disappeared — because the Russian people were forced to eat them. Ballet master George Balanchine was then a young dance student. When he could, he stole food to survive. He once had a job where he was paid in coffee grounds and potato peelings. When Mr. Balanchine left Russia in 1924, he took notice of what he saw on the tables in the dining room of the steamer he was sailing on: "It was such a beautiful sight — all that beautiful bread just sitting there like that, so casually, with no one guarding it — I almost wept."[110]

• A starving dervish passed through a village where no one would feed him. However, he heard that a wealthy man was dying, so he announced that if someone would take him to the wealthy man, he would save a life. At the wealthy man's side, the starving dervish said a prayer for the wealthy man's soul, then dined on good food. After the wealthy man died, members of the household asked the dervish to explain why he had reneged on his promise to save a life. "But I did save a life," replied the well-fed dervish. "I saved my own."[111]

• British character actress Margaret Rutherford had clout as a result of becoming internationally famous in movies such as *Blithe Spirit*. Whenever she made a movie, filming stopped at 11 a.m. and at 3:30 p.m. so that she could have her snack — hot milk and buttered cookies. According to *Time* magazine, Ms. Rutherford — a heavy woman — "needs the sustenance as much as a lush needs booze."[112]

• When comedian Bob Smith first moved to New York City, he — like so many other creative people — worked as a cater-waiter, one of whose fringe benefits is to eat the same food as the people they are serving. This meant that he ate such things as "radicchio, caviar, risotto, and chocolate truffles." According to Mr. Smith, in New York starving artists can eat quite well.[113]

• As a young man trying to break into the music scene in New York City with four friends, Duke Ellington found the going tough. Sometimes, he and his four fellow musicians were forced to cut a hot dog into five pieces so everyone could have a bite to keep off starvation.[114]

• Lots of people think comedians become comedians because they have a need for love and for recognition. Phyllis Diller says she became a comedienne because of a need for food. Poverty is what drove her to make people laugh — she points out, "Everybody has to eat."[115]

• When children's book writer Phyllis Reynolds Naylor was a little girl, she worried about The Last Judgment. Thinking that the lines of people waiting to be judged would be very long, she carried two butter cookies in her pocket in case she got hungry.[116]

• Quaker pastor Stan Banker knows a Quaker restaurant that is excellent, although he wonders if confusion may someday result because this sign is placed rather too close to the restrooms: "Welcome, Friend, Will Thee Please Wait to be Seated?"[117]

• Comedian Beatrice Lillie despised pretension. Often, she would go to a fancy restaurant filled with haughty headwaiters, then make her order: "Rice Krispies."[118]

• Yogi Berra was once asked if he wanted his pizza cut into four slices, or eight. He replied, "Four. I don't think I can eat eight slices."[119]

Friends

• After Shannon Miller won five medals as an Olympic gymnast in Barcelona, she flew on to Washington, D.C., to meet several political VIPs. However, several people greeted her parents at the Oklahoma City airport when they arrived back in their home state. Among them were some people who worked with Claudia Miller, Shannon's mother. They wore pajamas and bedroom slippers — because, they claimed, they wanted her to recognize the sacrifice they had made to come to the airport so late.[120]

• Ben Hecht and Charles MacArthur were friends and writing collaborators. They liked to play board games together and bet on the outcome. However, Mr. MacArthur habitually lost, complained about cheating, and never paid Mr. Hecht. Whenever the total amount of money he owed to Mr. Hecht reached $100,000, Mr. MacArthur would take out a $5 bill from his wallet, lay it on the table, and say, "Tear up that crooked score, and we'll start playing for cash."[121]

• Irish playwright Brendan Behan was sitting in a London pub and speaking Gaelic with a lot of his friends when the porter said to him, "Speak English and stop making a show of yourself." Mr. Behan said later, "You can judge for yourself the reply he got from me in the mellifluous tongue of Shakespeare, Milton, and Johnson."[122]

• A Jew complained to Rabbi Isaac Meir that in all the world, he didn't have a friend. Rabbi Isaac replied, "Surely you have a *Gemara* in your house?" (A *Gemara* is a part of the Talmud and consists of commentary on the Mishnah.)[123]

Gifts

• Music-hall comedian Alec Finlay was a practical joker. When his friend Jimmy Logan wanted to use his dressing room, Mr. Finlay let him, but when Mr. Logan entered the dressing room, he discovered that large padlocks were on all the cases and every drawer and wardrobe had been tied shut with thick rope. However, Mr. Logan got revenge. A couple of nights later, he had an orchestra play "Happy Birthday" for Mr. Finlay, and he sent him 12 gift-boxes — but the "gifts" were Mr. Finlay's own padlocks and rope.[124]

• Like other satirists, Mort Sahl was angry and he wanted other people to be angry. (Certainly we have enough things to be angry about, and getting angry about them may result in change.) He once advised, "You know what I want you to do? I want you to blow out the candles and curse the darkness." Mr. Sahl was a good friend of jazz musician Paul Desmond, a sax player. Mr. Sahl once gave Mr. Desmond a cigarette lighter inscribed, "To the sound from the fury."[125]

God

• At the 1965 Bing Crosby National Pro-Am, Matt Palacio hooked a drive toward the ocean. Disgusted with himself, he told bystanders, "Only God can save that one." The ocean waves receded as the ball fell, and the ball hit a rock and bounced back on the fairway. Mr. Palacio said, "Thank you, God."[126]

• If you want to achieve a love of God, what can you do? Does a magic charm exist that will help you to love God? According to R.

Judah Zevi of Stretyn, the answer is yes: "The best aid for achieving love of God is love of man."[127]

• A German mother taught her daughter how to pray by telling her to say, "Thank God for Adolf Hitler." Her daughter asked, "What should I say if Hitler dies?" The mother replied, "Then just say, 'Thank God.'"[128]

• Justice Oliver Wendell Holmes could be humble. When he was asked which principle he used in forming his judicial opinions, he replied, "I have spent 70 years finding out that I am not God."[129]

• During an earthquake in Los Angeles, Pat McCormick telephoned a friend of his to joke, "The God is Dead Rally has been cancelled."[130]

Good Deeds

• James M. Barrie was the author of *Peter Pan*. His wife, Mary, fell out of love with him, and she asked for a divorce. The divorce laws were harsh at that time, as they required proof that his wife had been unfaithful to him. The divorce would have created a terrific scandal, but several of Mr. Barrie's friends — including H.G. Wells, Henry James, A.E.W. Mason, and Beerbohm Tree — requested that the newspapers keep it quiet. Mr. Barrie forgave her. Later, Mary's second marriage ended, and she was desperate for money, so Mr. Barrie gave her an allowance for the rest of her life.[131]

• During the 1950s, an old man knocked on a door at Lancashire School and asked the two schoolboys who answered his knock if he could sit down in the room as he believed that long ago he had lived in this room at the school. After they had entertained the old man and he had left, the schoolboys were astonished to learn that their visitor had been the world-famous conductor Sir Thomas Beecham, who had attended Lancashire School as a teenager.[132]

• The great dancer Bill Robinson, aka Mr. Bojangles, organized a benefit that had the first mixed — black and white — audience in Miami, Florida, history. Money raised from the benefit helped underprivileged black children and was administered by the NAACP. Mr. Robinson insisted that blacks be allowed to attend. They were.[133]

Heaven and Hell

• As a boy, H. Allen Smith was raised Catholic, but unknown to his Catholic friends, he sometimes also attended a Protestant church. One day, he asked the sexton of the Catholic Church if a person could be a member of a Catholic church and a Protestant church at the same time. The sexton took him to the basement of the Catholic church, opened the door to the furnace, and told him to look inside at the burning coals. Then the sexton said, "That there is *ice cold* alongside the hell you would go to if you so much as set foot in a Protestant church. That there is ice cold alongside the hell the Protestants go to. Don't never go in no Protestant church." Young H. Allen stopped attending the Protestant church.[134]

• American bass Henri Scott once played Mephistopheles in a European production of *Faust*. Unfortunately, as he was descending into Hell through a stage trapdoor, his sword was situated in such a way that it prevented him from descending more than halfway. A member of the audience called out, "Look! Hell must be full — there is no room even for the devil!"[135]

• Art Linkletter used to interview children on TV. He asked one little boy what was the best way to get to Heaven. The little boy answered, "Die."[136]

Husbands and Wives

• As a young minister, Chuck Terrill was finding it hard to fit into his church and feel comfortable with the members of the congregation. Fortunately, one Sunday he preached a sermon on different kinds of love, including *agape*, *phileo*, and *eros*. During the sermon, he asked if anyone in the congregation could give him an example of any of these kinds of love. His own daughter, four-and-a-half-year-old Sarah, raised her hand. He asked, "Sarah, can you give us an example of one of these types of love?" She nodded her head yes, then she said, "Sometimes, my

Mommy takes a shower with my Daddy." The congregation had a good laugh, the ice between pastor and congregation was broken, and Pastor Terrill was able to begin doing authentic, loving ministry.[137]

• President Lyndon B. Johnson once met with evangelist Billy Graham and his wife, Ruth. During the meeting, President Johnson handed Mr. Graham a list of 14 names and asked which of the 14 he would recommend as a running mate. However, Mrs. Graham objected that her husband should dispense spiritual advice only and not political advice. President Johnson told her, "Ruth, that's exactly right." But after Mrs. Graham had left the room, President Johnson asked her husband, "All right, now what do you *really* think?"[138]

• Sir John Barbirolli was interested most of all in the performance of his orchestra. Once, the wife of one of his musicians came to him with a problem — her husband was seeing another, younger woman. Sir John thought for a moment, then he told her, "Things are not all that bad, you know. After all, he is playing better than ever."[139]

• Shortly after Edmund Hillary had become one of the two first men to climb to the top of Mount Everest — an achievement for which he was knighted — he married Louise Rose. At their wedding, the happy couple departed from the church by passing under an archway constructed of ice axes.[140]

Illnesses and Injuries

• When she was a teenager, children's mystery writer Joan Lowery Nixon fell from a horse and suffered a fractured skull. Her sister, Pat, was attending a Catholic school and asked the nuns to pray for Joan. Shortly before the nuns were to begin praying for her, Joan fell into a deep sleep despite an incessant headache, and she dreamed that her late grandfather stroked her forehead. When she woke up, her headache was gone and she was very quickly well again. Later, Joan met one of the nuns who had prayed for her. The nun pointed out, "You were healed when we prayed for you." This was true, and the nun speculated, "You received a message from God. You must listen and look within yourself. I believe that God wants you to become a nun." However, Joan had recently discovered the wonderful world of cute boys, so she replied, "I'm not sure what message God gave me. Maybe he wants me to become the mother of a bishop."[141]

• Joe Garagiola once had the "opportunity" to bat against the very good pitcher Ewell Blackwell, and he was sure that his .212 batting average would drop to .199 by the end of the game. Fortunately, two close friends of his, Father Boul and Father Scheffer, had the cure for a batting slump. Father Boul doused Mr. Garagiola with holy water, saying, "Straight from Lourdes — that means at least two hits." And Father Scheffer gave Mr. Garagiola a heavy crucifix to put in his back pocket for another two hits. At first, the religious help seemed to work. Mr. Garagiola hit a high fastball, and he slid safely into second base. Unfortunately, he slid on the crucifix, which gave him a six-inch gash in a spot where no tourniquet could be applied. The trainer, Doc Weaver, asked Mr. Garagiola, "What in the world happened?" Mr. Garagiola gave him an honest answer: "God just helped me."[142]

• Franklin Delano Roosevelt's mother could be quite demanding, but he learned how to get his way by seeming to agree with her yet doing something to get his own way. For example, his mother wanted him to go to church, so he used to get headaches on Sunday mornings and skip going to church; remarkably, the headaches were always gone in the afternoon when church was over. His parents even gave the headaches a name — they were young Franklin's "Sunday headaches."[143]

• Golfer Bob Jones suffered in his later years from syringomyelia, a degenerative disease of the spinal cord. In 1971, at the Augusta National, an old friend visited him in his cabin. Unfortunately, Mr. Jones' illness had taken a heavy toll on him, and his friend saw this and started to cry. Mr. Jones, however, was very accepting of his disease, and he told his friend, "Now, now. We won't have that. We are supposed to play our ball as we find it."[144]

• Comedy writers Goodman Ace and Al Boasberg once went to the movies together. In the middle of the movie, Mr. Boasberg stood up and asked loudly, "Is there a Christian Scientist in the house?" A woman replied that she was, and asked, "What do you want?" Mr. Boasberg replied, "Would you mind changing seats with me? I'm sitting in a draft."[145]

Marriage

• Many women dream of having the perfect wedding, but Erma Bombeck's wedding was not perfect. When Erma Fiste walked down the aisle to wed Bill Bombeck, she noticed a spot of white paint on his ear and she smelled turpentine. (Mr. Bombeck used to paint houses to supplement his income.) When she heard the priest say that Bill was to be the head of the house, and she was to be its heart, she thought, "In your dreams!" Later, when the couple arrived at the wilderness cabin where they were to spend their honeymoon, they saw bear traps outside the cabin. (They stayed happily married until Ms. Bombeck died in April of 1996.)[146]

• In *Loving v. Virginia*, a biracial couple went to the United States Supreme Court in a successful attempt to force the state of Virginia to legally recognize their marriage. Many Roman Catholic bishops supported the Lovings, and they submitted a brief to the Supreme Court. In the brief, they argued that marriage is a sacrament of the church, and as such, being able to marry a consenting adult of your choice is a "free exercise of religion."[147]

• A Scottish minister with a sense of humor — or reality — used to say this to young couples he was about to marry: "My friends, marriage is a blessing to a few, a curse to many, and a great uncertainty to all — do ye venture?"[148]

• Brigham Young brought Mormonism, which permitted bigamy — a fact of which Mr. Young took full advantage — to Utah. According to Artemus Ward, "The girls in Utah mostly marry Young."[149]

Chapter 4: From Mishaps to Prayer

Mishaps

• Judges in figure skating can honestly make mistakes. While judging an event, Morry Stillwell was watching skater Christopher Bowman and taking notes when his pencil broke. He reached for another pencil, taking his eyes away from the skater for a very brief time, then turned his eyes back upon the skater. However, after the program was finished and the judges' scores were posted, Mr. Stillwell saw that his scores were way above all the other judges' scores. Shocked, he asked another judge, "What happened?" The other judge replied, "He hit the wall, you dumb ****."[150]

• Comedy writer Goodman Ace once wrote down several jokes, then looked in a 100-year-old book of jokes to see if it would inspire some new ideas. However, he found in the book a joke that he thought he had just written. Because of this experience, Mr. Ace believes that no matter what comedic idea you have, "somewhere, somebody must've thought of it before."[151]

• A hearing-able man once started to communicate with a deaf woman by writing messages on paper. Later, another hearing-able man joined the conversation, also writing messages on paper. Soon, the deaf woman left, but the two men continued their paper-and-pen conversation because neither of them realized that the other could hear.[152]

• Jimmy Walker, the Mayor of New York City, once had a photo op with some reindeer herders and their dogs. He wore a fur coat to the photo op, and the largest dog jumped up on him, sniffed, and then began to bark with joy. Afterwards, Mr. Walker asked, "Which did the dog recognize as his brother — the coat or me?"[153]

• Comedian Bob Newhart once owned an ancient Greek vase that he loved to touch. Unfortunately, his children also loved to touch it.

Ironically, this ancient Greek vase that had been unbroken for over 2,000 years lasted only about two years in Mr. Newhart's house before his children broke it.[154]

• Merce Cunningham and his dancers once gave a performance at Notre Dame on the same day of a prom. Exactly 16 people attended their performance — six were priests and 10 were nuns.[155]

• Senator Austin Warren once tried to mediate peace between the Israelis and the Arabs at the United Nations. He said, "Now, let's all try to settle this problem in a true Christian manner."[156]

Money

• An impoverished cobbler once complained to R. Ezekiel that whenever he worked a little too long, continuing his work into the Sabbath, his neighbors reproached him. On the other hand, the factories of the richest Jew in town continued to be busy all during the Sabbath with chimneys belching smoke into the air, and no one ever reproached the rich Jew. R. Ezekiel explained that the cobbler's neighbors were looking out for him. Because the cobbler was poor, he was not able to enjoy many of the good things of this world. The rich Jew, on the other hand, because he was rich, was able to enjoy many of the good things of this world. Therefore, R. Ezekiel said, "That rich Jew enjoys this world, and if by desecrating the Sabbath he loses the world to come, at least he has something. But it is different with you. If you remain working after the holy Sabbath has begun, you will be in danger of losing both worlds."[157]

• One of the things that Henny Youngman learned in his many decades as a comedian is *nem di gelt* — Yiddish for "take the money." Once he was hired at fabulous pay to perform before 6,500 people at the Waldorf-Astoria in New York. After his performance, he took the elevator to the lobby, but mistakenly got off on the second floor. In the hallway of the second floor, he noticed a sign for a bar mitzvah in a certain room, so he went to the room, talked to the father of the boy (soon to be a man) to see if he could entertain, and very happily made another $150 (small change in comparison to what he had just made upstairs). The father got a good deal: Mr. Youngman did exactly the same act that he had just done upstairs at fabulous pay.[158]

• Comedian Lenny Bruce used to tell his audiences about the time Jesus and Moses returned to Earth, walked around, and finally ended up in St. Patrick's Cathedral in New York City, where they saw Francis Cardinal Spellman. They weren't impressed with what they saw; instead, they wondered why Cardinal Spellman was wearing an $8,000 ring when they had just seen 40 Puerto Ricans crammed into a one-room apartment.[159]

• Comedian Bill Hicks and his comedian friends loved to watch such religious programs as *The PTL* [*Praise the Lord* and *People That Love*] *Club*. They used to make bets about how long it would take the preacher to stop talking about Jesus and start talking about dollars.[160]

Movies

• When Monty Python's Flying Circus first came up with the idea to make a film about the beginning of Christianity, its members thought at first that they would make fun of Jesus. However, university graduates all, they read the New Testament gospels and other sources carefully, developed a great respect for Jesus, and made their film *The Life of Brian* not about Jesus, but about a character who supposedly lived at the same time as Jesus. Nevertheless, the film was controversial and some people described it as a "crime against religion." However, Python member Graham Chapman asked, "Don't they realize that God has a sense of humor?"[161]

• Edna Ferber was displeased by what *The New Yorker* wrote about a movie that was based on one of her novels, so she wrote Harold Ross, "Will you kindly inform the moron who runs your motion picture department that I did not write the motion picture entitled *Classified*? ... Also inform him that Moses did not write the motion picture entitled *The Ten Commandments*."[162]

• Making a movie takes teamwork — from many members of a team. Occasionally, a writer would complain to producer Louis B. Mayer because other people were changing the writer's work. Mr. Mayer would reply, "The number one book of the ages was written by a committee, and it was called The Bible."[163]

Music

• When rocker Bruce Springsteen was young, his parents worried about him because they felt that playing music was OK as a hobby but would not make a good career. Therefore, Mr. Springsteen went to Heaven to ask God what he should do with his life; in particular, he asked if he should stop playing music. God, who was sitting behind a set of drums, answered his question by saying, "What those guys don't understand is that there was supposed to be an Eleventh Commandment. All it said was this: "LET IT ROCK!"[164]

• Opera singer Leo Slezak's son, Walter, toyed with the idea of becoming a composer. Unfortunately, he was not a very good composer. Once, he wrote a flute solo that was 64 bars long. His music teacher examined the solo, then asked, "When does the flute player breathe?" On another occasion, he tried to write an opera titled *Nero*, which opened with Nero fiddling while Rome burned. Unfortunately, Walter didn't know what to write to follow such an exciting beginning.[165]

• Young, impoverished musicians sometimes made musical instruments out of cigar boxes. Blues singer Big Bill Broonzy made a fiddle out of a cigar box when he was 10 years old and played it until a friend gave him a real fiddle. Another blues singer, Big Joe Williams, whose professional name was Poor Joe, made a guitar out of a cigar box and played it until he got a real guitar at age 15.[166]

• Jack Benny used a violin as a stage prop — and to hide his stage fright. According to his friend George Burns, Mr. Benny was "frightened that if he didn't hold on to something he'd fall down." Once, Mr. Benny forgot his violin, walked on stage, told two usually surefire jokes that didn't get laughs, and then was forced to borrow a violin from the orchestra leader so he could continue his act.[167]

• Author Maurice Maeterlinck once tried to take a photograph of opera singer Mary Garden, saying, "Come into my dark room. I want to photograph your soul." However, Ms. Garden demurred and replied, "I should say not. Everything about me the world seems to own. That is the only thing that belongs to me and I can't let it go on a plate."[168]

• Ludwig van Beethoven's creation of the *Missa Solemnis* caused him to lose two servants. According to his secretary Anton Schindler, Beethoven stayed behind closed doors, "singing, howling, and stamping his foot" in an attempt to get the "Credo" fugue right. Two maids were so frightened that they quit.[169]

• Ludwig van Beethoven wrote music that is difficult to play. When a violinist, Ignaz Schuppanzigh, complained to him about a particularly difficult passage in a string quartet, Beethoven shouted, "I CAN'T THINK ABOUT YOUR MISERABLE VIOLIN WHEN I AM SPEAKING TO MY GOD."[170]

• Sir Thomas Beecham once was displeased with the way the chorus was singing a passage in *Messiah*, and so he asked, "When we sing, 'All we like sheep have gone astray,' might we, please, have a little more regret and a little less satisfaction?"[171]

• The famed conductor Sir Thomas Beecham whistled in a New York taxi until an annoyed companion asked him to stop whistling. Sir Thomas replied, "You can only hear my whistling. I can hear the full orchestra."[172]

• Sir Thomas Beecham once rehearsed an orchestra in Canterbury Cathedral. During the rehearsal, a leader of his orchestra propped his feet on the high altar — so Sir Thomas fired him.[173]

• Baseball great Yogi Berra once attended the opera *Tosca* with his wife, Carmen. She asked if he had enjoyed the opera, and Mr. Berra replied, "I really liked it. Even the music was good."[174]

• Leonard Bernstein's *Mass* called for a huge cast of singers, narrators, musicians, and dancers. When it was first performed in 1971, Mr. Bernstein kissed each of its 200 performers.[175]

Names

• Ira Dutton, who wished to be called Brother Joseph despite not being a member of any order of Catholics, aided Father Damien in his service to the lepers at Molokai. Early in his life, Mr. Dutton had been an alcoholic, and after recovering he felt that he had wasted part of his life and wished to make amends. He converted to Catholicism, and in a convent library, he read about Father Damien. Mr. Dutton went to Molokai, and after Father Damien died, Mr. Dutton continued to care for the lepers. A layman once asked Mr. Dutton why he wished to be called Brother Joseph. He replied, "Because I want to be a brother to everybody."[176]

• Dorothy Parker had a tart tongue. She once said, "That woman speaks eighteen languages, and she can't say 'no' in any of them." When an acquaintance left the table, saying he had to "go take a leak," Ms. Parker remarked, "He really wants to telephone, but he's too embarrassed to say so." And when she was being shown an apartment available to rent, she remarked, "Oh, dear, that's much too big. All I need is room enough to lay a hat and a few friends." Her comment on a prom at Princeton was, "If all the girls were laid end to end, I wouldn't be surprised." And she named her canary "Onan" because "it scatters its seed."[177]

• Franklin Delano Roosevelt was a reporter for and editor of the Harvard *Crimson*. Once, he used his connections to get a scoop. His fifth cousin was Teddy Roosevelt, and when Teddy was Vice President of the United States, he came to Harvard to lecture in a certain class. Franklin printed the time and place of the lecture, and 2,000 people showed up for the lecture. By the way, on March 17 — St. Patrick's Day — of 1905, Franklin Roosevelt married Eleanor Roosevelt. Franklin's fifth cousin, Teddy Roosevelt, told him, "There's nothing like keeping the name in the family."[178]

• Harpo Marx's name at birth was Adolph Marx, but because of Hitler, he legally changed his name to Arthur Marx. When Harpo died at age 70 in 1964, Groucho wrote about him in a letter to Betty Comden: "Having worked with Harpo for forty years, which is much longer than most marriages last, his death left quite a void in my life. He was worth all the wonderful adjectives that were used to describe him. He was a nice man in the fullest sense of the word. He loved life and lived it joyously and deeply, and that's about as good an epitaph as anyone can have."[179]

• Mary Elfrieda Scruggs Bailey married John Williams and became Mary Williams. When she began to record as a jazz pianist, her agent wanted her to have a better name, so he added Lou to her name, and she became Mary Lou Williams — the name that jazz fans know her by. Later, she converted to Roman Catholicism and began to compose church music. When she established a foundation to help struggling musicians, she named it Bel Canto — the name, which is Italian, means "Beautiful Singing."[180]

• Mozart's full name at birth was Johannes Chrysostomus Wolfgangus Theophilus Mozart, but he later changed "Theophilus" to "Amadeus." Both names mean "beloved of God." By the way, while touring as a very young boy and music prodigy, Mozart proposed marriage to Marie Antoinette. She declined.[181]

• Craig McNair Wilson has a theory about how angels got their name. It happened when Adam had just spent a day in the Garden of Eden naming things. Tired and thirsty, he turned to a being of light near him and requested, "Be an angel and get me something to drink."[182]

Nuns

• Mother Teresa started the Missionaries of Charity and turned it into an international organization. In San Francisco, she inspected a house for members of the Missionaries of Charity and was unhappy with what she saw — the house was too luxurious. Therefore, she ordered that such "luxuries" as carpeting and bedsprings be taken away, explaining, "For us to be able to understand the poor, we must know what poverty is."[183]

• As a famous comedian, Phyllis Diller sometimes resorted to trickery to guard her privacy. For a while, she travelled incognito. She dressed as a nun, complete with a habit, no makeup, and rimless glasses. One day she laughed, and her fellow passengers recognized her famous cackle and thus discovered her identity.[184]

• Catholic nuns take vows of poverty, chastity, and obedience. However, when Mother Teresa started the Missionaries of Charity, she added a fourth vow for nuns in her organization: To do these things with joy.[185]

People with Handicaps

• George Jessel used to tell a story about the banker Otto Kahn and Marshall P. Wilder (who possessed a ready wit and who was a person with a hunchback). The two men were walking down the street. When they passed a famous Christian church, Mr. Kahn pointed it out and said that he was now a member. "Why, Mr. Kahn, I thought you were a Jew," Mr. Wilder said. "I was, but I changed," Mr. Kahn replied. A few moments later, Mr. Marshall said, "You know, I used to be a hunchback."[186]

• When two deaf people are arguing and one person gets tired of the argument, all she has to do to end the argument is to close her eyes. It is up to the other person to figure out how to get her to open her eyes so the argument can continue.[187]

Practical Jokes

• At Cornell, an architecture professor worried that a crack in the ceiling of his lecture room would someday develop into a fallen ceiling. One day, he walked into the lecture room and saw that his fear had been realized — a big hole was in the ceiling, and chunks of plaster were lying on the floor. The professor rushed out to get some maintenance workers. When he returned with them, they saw only the regular crack in the ceiling — no gaping hole and no chunks of plaster on the floor. Here's what had happened. Hugh Troy, an architecture student at Cornell, knew of the professor's worries, so he had created a painting of a hole and even made it three-dimensional by gluing bits of plaster to the edges of the "hole." Mr. Troy fastened the painting to the ceiling at night, and put chunks of plaster on the floor, then after the professor had discovered that the ceiling had "fallen" and left to get help, Mr. Troy cleaned up the mess and removed the painting.[188]

• While in Canada, Anna Russell was invited to live on a farm with her Aunt Alice — and Uncle Ern, whom she had never met. Arriving at the farm, she discovered that Aunt Alice was gone, but she had a nice talk with a man who said he was her gardener. He gave her a lecture on plants and keeping a compost pile, and he certainly knew a lot about gardening. When Ms. Russell asked how long he had been working for her Aunt Alice, he replied, "Man and boy, fifty year. She be a right fine lady to work for." However, Ms. Russell was shocked when her Aunt Alice came home and gave the gardener a kiss. The mystery was explained when Aunt Alice said, "Hello, Ern," then introduced Ms. Russell to her practical joker of a husband.[189]

• In the musical *Dreamgirls* is a scene in which the actors and actresses pretend to be playing musical instruments. One actress whom Derryl Yeager disliked did not want to mess up her lipstick, so she always put the mouthpiece of her French horn not on her lips, but on her nose, reasoning that the audience was far enough away that they wouldn't notice. Mr. Yeager decided to play a practical joke on the actress, so he filled up the mouthpiece of the French horn with toothpaste. The actress definitely noticed the toothpaste when she pulled the French horn away from her nose — and suddenly a string of white goo appeared dangling between the French horn and her nose.[190]

• Charlie Chaplin enjoyed performing for other people — more than he enjoyed being a ladies man. One day, Sid Grauman of Grauman's Chinese Theater in Hollywood decided to play a trick on Mr. Chaplin. Mr. Grauman borrowed a realistic female mannikin, dressed it in a negligee, and installed it in a hotel bed. Mr. Grauman then told Mr. Chaplin that a female admirer of his wanted to meet him, and he told Mr. Chaplin at which hotel room he could meet her. Mr. Chaplin arrived, and immediately began to perform for what he thought was a real-live woman. Not until 30 minutes had passed did Mr. Chaplin discover that he was performing for a mannikin.[191]

• John Salkeld was an English Quaker as well as a man who enjoyed humor. This worried his more serious Quaker friends, who decided to talk to him about what they felt was his joking to excess. They stayed at his house a long time to talk to Mr. Salkeld, who left them for a few minutes, then hurried back to tell them excitedly, "Friends, come at once. My wife is speechless." They ran into the room where she was, only to discover that she was sound asleep.[192]

• Jimmy Durante was superstitious and believed that placing a hat on a bed brought bad luck and the only way to stop the bad luck was first, to hang up the hat, and second, for the owner to wear another hat before touching the first hat. One day, some friends played a practical joke on him. They placed 25 hats on Mr. Durante's bed in a hotel and then hid in the bathroom to watch his reaction.[193]

• In his high school chemistry class, Joel Perry spilled a harmless liquid on classmate Betty Swails, then told her it was hydrochloric acid. She screamed as she ran to the lab's safety shower and soaked both herself and the teacher's desk.[194]

Prayer

• Baltimore Oriole Pat Kelly was deeply religious, married a minister's daughter, and went to chapel before games. In a game he batted with the bases loaded and with three balls and two strikes already called, but unfortunately he swung at a pitch that was an obvious ball — and so he struck out instead of walking. After going to chapel the next day, Mr. Kelly told his manager, Earl Weaver, "I feel great. I've just left the chapel, and once again I've learned to walk with the Lord." Mr. Weaver said, "Too bad you didn't learn to walk with the bases loaded." Mr. Kelly then asked, "When's the last time you got down on your knees and prayed?" Mr. Weaver replied, "The last time I sent you up to pinch hit."[195]

• A farmer walked into a restaurant and sat down and placed his order. Unfortunately, a group of rowdies came in, making noise, ordering servers around, and generally behaving like jerks. When the farmer's order arrived, he bowed his head and prayed, and the leader of the rowdies asked him, "Where you come from, does everyone do that?" The farmer replied, "No, not everyone — the pigs don't."[196]

• When dancer Rudolf Nureyev was growing up in Ufa, food was scarce. In the cabin where he lived was an elderly Christian couple who promised to give him food if he would rise early and pray with them. In later life, Mr. Nureyev said, "It was dark and I was very sleepy — but more hungry than sleepy." Young Rudolf prayed with the elderly Christian couple.[197]

• When Helen Ross was dying of cancer, her friend Fred Rogers (TV's Mister Rogers) visited her. She asked him, "Do you ever pray for people, Fred?" He replied, "Of course I do: Dear God, encircle us with Thy love wherever we may be." She said, "That's what it's all about, isn't it? It's love. That's what it's all about."[198]

• The Western Mono Native American tribe gather sticks to weave into baskets. After they gather the materials to be used to make baskets, they thank the Creator and the plants and the earth for what they have taken. They are also careful not to take so much that they prevent the vegetation from growing back.[199]

• Part of the Kinaaldá ceremony that marks a Navajo girl's coming of age is a night of prayers in which the girl stays up all night and is introduced to the Holy People — spiritual beings who can help her during her life.[200]

 • At a concert, an audience once greeted conductor Sir Thomas Beecham with complete silence. Sir Thomas looked at the audience, then turned to his orchestra and said, "Let us pray."[201]

 • Adlai Stevenson's favorite prayer was from St. Francis of Assisi: "Let me be an instrument of Thy peace."[202]

Chapter 5: From Preachers to Work

Preachers

• After Dr. Martin Luther King, Jr., electrified the congregation at a Baptist church, someone asked his wife, Coretta Scott King, if Dr. King were always that good a speaker. She replied, "Sometimes he's even better."[203]

• President Abraham Lincoln once saw a small boy making a church out of mud. President Lincoln asked why the boy why he didn't also make a preacher, and the boy replied, "I ain't got mud enough."[204]

Prejudice

• In 1895, Theodore Roosevelt was Police Commissioner in New York City. Rector Ahlwardt, an anti-Semitic preacher, came to New York to lead a rally against the Jews, and many New York Jews appealed to Mr. Roosevelt to stop Rector Ahlwardt from speaking. Of course, in the United States the First Amendment protects free speech, including unpopular speech, so Mr. Roosevelt could not stop Rector Ahlwardt from speaking — and therefore he made him look ridiculous. He assigned 40 policemen and a police sergeant — all Jews — to protect Rector Ahlwardt. As Rector Ahlwardt criticized the Jews in his anti-Semitic speech, he was surrounded by Jews, all of whom were protecting him.[205]

• During the heyday of the Borsch Belt, the training ground for many, many famous Jewish comedians, anti-Semitism was still prevalent in much of America. The Jewish vacation resort Totem Lodge was located 12 miles from Albany, New York, and occasionally anti-Semites would get together, construct a cross on a boat, set the cross on fire, then send it across the lake to the Jewish resort. The Jews got tired of this, so one night they waited for the anti-Semites. After the anti-Semites got out of the hospital, they decided not to burn any more crosses.[206]

• In junior high school, Brian Wright, who was later a famous choreographer in figure skating, was teased without mercy because he was a figure skater. Boys taunted him, telling him, "You're a figure skater. You're a fairy. Brian is a fairy." Even at age 13, he knew he was different from the other boys — they were falling in love with girls, while he was falling in love with Bruce Lee, an actor who was then appearing in TV's *Green Hornet* — so he faced the boys calling him a fairy and with scorn in his voice screamed at them, "YES, I AM!"[207]

• The late Monty Python member Graham Chapman once appeared on a TV talk show, in which he discussed his homosexuality. A viewer wrote in to the talk show, enclosing in her letter some prayers for Chapman's soul, as well as the biblical injunction that if a man lie with another he shall be taken out and killed. Python leader Eric Idle read the viewer's letter, then wrote her in reply, "We've taken him out and killed him!" (Fortunately, not all Christians are against homosexuals. Many Christians are loving people — as they should be.)[208]

• Some folks feel threatened by female pastors. Joel Perry's brother became pastor of a Methodist church in North Carolina after its mostly elderly members became upset when a female pastor was sent to them. Within six months after he arrived, he had buried six elderly members of the church. Joel believes that the elderly members had clung to life just so they could be buried by a male pastor.[209]

• Blues singer William "Big Bill" Lee Conley Broonzy was born during the days of Jim Crow, and all of his family suffered from prejudice. His grandmother was bi-racial, and when she married a black man, her family wanted nothing to do with her. When Big Bill was a boy, he used to walk her to church, but he couldn't go inside because his skin wasn't light enough. Instead, he waited outside for church to end, then he walked his grandmother home.[210]

• Jack Benny was Jewish, and Eddie "Rochester" Anderson was African-American. One of their comedy writers was Texan John Tackaberry, who once put down a bigot making offensive remarks in his presence by saying, "I make my living writing for Jack Benny and Rochester and I'm here to tell you that I never met two finer people, so I don't want to hear no more nasty remarks about n*ggers and k*kes."[211]

• Benjamin Franklin was famous for his literary hoaxes. While in London, he once read aloud a passage that he said was a chapter from Genesis, but which was in fact from his own pen. Mr. Franklin's "chapter from Genesis" praised tolerance and told a story about Abraham being rebuked by God because Abraham had punished a stranger who had refused to worship God.[212]

• An old Jew was surrounded by Nazis who asked him, "Who is the cause of all of Germany's problems?" The old Jew replied, "The Jews — and the bicyclists." The Nazis asked, "Why the bicyclists?" The old Jew replied, "Why the Jews?"[213]

Problem-Solving

• Tanka, a Zen master, once waited at a Buddhist temple for the priest to return. While waiting, he grew cold. Noticing that the temple housed three wooden statues of Buddha, he chopped up the largest statue and made a fire from its pieces. Just then, the priest returned. Seeing the fire, he exclaimed, "What are you doing?" Tanka replied, "I am burning the body of the Buddha so I can find the bones and save them as relics." "That is a wooden statue," said the priest. "Don't you know that you won't find bones in wood?" "In that case," Tanka replied, seizing the other two statues and throwing them on the fire, "we might as well burn these Buddhas, too."[214]

• A thief robbed the house of a dervish at night, but had the misfortune to awaken the dervish and so took off running for home while carrying half of the dervish's possessions. The dervish saw the thief running off, recognized him, and so he grabbed more of his possessions and followed the thief to the thief's house. "What are you doing?" cried the thief when he saw the dervish at his front doorstep. The dervish replied, "You have been so kind to move half of my possessions to a better dwelling, so I am moving the other half. Tomorrow morning my wife and seven children will move in, too." The thief immediately returned the dervish's possessions.[215]

• Hugh Troy had an aunt whom he considered officious. Once, she arrived for a visit while his parents were out of town, so he and his sister prepared for her visit by bringing down several pieces of furniture from the attic to the living room. After eating supper, the officious aunt was sitting in the living room when Hugh and his sister arrived carrying hatchets and loudly discussing the furniture, saying that there was way too much and that it was always getting in their way. Then they started chopping up the furniture and carrying it out of the house. The aunt returned to her home the next morning.[216]

• Ellen Orleans and her lesbian lover, Lori, were staying at an inn near Aspen. They put on their swimsuits for a romantic time in the hot tub but were disappointed to see it already occupied by a man and a woman, so they went to the pool and played games such as Ellen pretending to be a shark and diving to bite Lori's toes. Then they went to the hot tub, occupied or not. The man and woman saw them coming and quickly got out of the tub, leaving Ellen and her lover alone, which is exactly what they wanted.[217]

• Joan Rivers was serious about getting work when she was a struggling young comedian. She once crawled on the floor with a rose in her mouth — a gift to the secretary of a booking agent. She would sometimes write in the appointment book of a secretary to a booking agent: "This is your last chance: Get Molinsky [Joan Rivers' real last name] a job or you'll be wearing cement booties."[218]

• Harry Marten (1602-1680) was known for frequently taking naps during debates in Parliament. When a Member of Parliament proposed that people who nodded off during debates should be turned out, Mr. Marten made a counterproposal: "Mr. Speaker, a motion has been made to turn out the nodders; I desire that the noddees may also be turned out."[219]

• American evangelist Dwight L. Moody had very good problem-solving skills. At a prayer meeting, a man started a very long prayer, and when the length of the prayer became excessive, Mr. Moody said to the worshippers, "While our brother finishes his prayer, let's sing a hymn." The worshippers sang, and the man's prayer quickly came to an end.[220]

• Thomas Beecham and his orchestra once had trouble passing through Irish customs, so they decided to do something to prove that they were harmless. Some members of the orchestra played "The Keel Row" and Mr. Beecham danced an Irish jig. The Irish music and dance greatly speeded their passage through customs.[221]

• Zen masters have always been very good problem-solvers. Once a kicking horse was in a street, and the villagers wondered what they should do about it. Finally, they decided to wait for the Zen master. The master walked into the street, saw the kicking horse, then turned and walked down a different street.[222]

• Some gay men have become very effective at protesting discrimination. For example, if a restaurant refuses to serve a couple simply because they are gay, the gay couple gathers a group of gay friends, then they descend upon the restaurant in a mass and hold a kiss-in.[223]

Profanity

• Actor Douglas Fairbanks enjoyed telling this story about a chaplain taking part in an amateur theatrical production in England. In the play, the chaplain was supposed to get shot and say, "My God! He has shot me!" However, the chaplain objected to saying "My God!" and instead proposed that he say, "My Goodness!" This was agreed to. On the night the play was to be given, at the last minute the property man did his bit for realism. He inserted a very ripe raspberry into the barrel of the villain's revolver, so it would create what would look like a bloodstain when the gun was fired. The play went on, the villain shot the chaplain, and the chaplain said, "My Goodness! He has shot me!" Then, noticing the raspberry "bloodstain" on his chest, the chaplain exclaimed, "My God! He *has* shot me!"[224]

• Groucho Marx was famous for — in addition to his appearances in Marx Brothers movies — his quiz show, *You Bet Your Life*. A sight gag on the show was that a duck wearing Groucho's trademark mustache, glasses, cigar, and bushy eyebrows dropped from the ceiling whenever someone said the "secret word" of the day. While vacationing in Rome, Groucho was jostled by someone, causing him to drop his cigar on the street. Groucho grumbled "God!" as he stooped to pick up his cigar. When he straightened up, a priest from Cleveland, Ohio, handed him two cigars and said, "Groucho, you just said the secret word!"[225]

• Football official Tom Thorp was a religious man, and he strongly disliked profanity. While he was officiating a game, one of the players kept using profanity although Mr. Thorp asked him not to, and finally Mr. Thorp threw him out of the game. The football player was angry and asked what rule he had broken, as did his coach and several of the players on his team. Mr. Thorp glared at them, then told them, "The Golden Rule."[226]

• Asa Branson, who originally hailed from Salem, New Jersey, but then moved to Flushing, Ohio, was an elderly Quaker who was hard of hearing and who therefore carried an ear trumpet. Some young men once tried to shock him by shouting profanity into his ear trumpet, but Mr. Branson responded by going to the nearby village pump and washing his ear trumpet.[227]

• In the middle of the last century, Cleburne (Texas) High School star player Jimmy Strickland asked his team to pray before a football game. However, after the kickoff the other football team started steadily advancing across the field, so Mr. Strickland told his fellow players during the huddle, "Men, some #$%$%@ didn't pray!"[228]

Public Speaking

• Lord Chesterfield was invited to attend a dinner that was given by the Spanish ambassador. At the dinner, several people gave toasts to their respective kings. The Spanish ambassador compared the King of Spain to the sun. The French ambassador compared the King of France to the moon. Next rose Lord Chesterfield, who said about the King of England, "Your excellencies have taken from me all the greatest luminaries of Heaven, and the stars are too small for me to make a comparison of my royal master; I therefore beg leave to give your excellencies — Joshua!" (Readers who know the Bible will remember that the great Hebrew military leader Joshua once stopped the sun and the moon, thus allowing the Israelites to win a battle before nightfall.)[229]

• Rev. M. Woolsey Stryker and two speakers were to dedicate a new church in Utica, New York. Because there were so many speakers, Rev. Stryker proposed that each limit himself to 20 minutes. The first speaker spoke for 30 minutes, but the second speaker spoke for 90 minutes. When it was his turn to speak, Rev. Stryker stood up, glared at the second speaker, then told the audience, "This congregation looks very much dedicated. So I will say nothing to you Uticans beyond suggesting that you all go home now and read that chapter in the New Testament which tells how Paul preached all night and Eutychus fell out of the window."[230]

• In *Acts*, chapter 20, we read that St. Paul spoke so long and so late that a young man named Eutychus, who was sitting in a third-story window, fell asleep. Eutychus fell out of the window and was killed. (Fortunately, through a miracle, he lived again.)[231]

Respect

• As a young English child growing up in India, Rumer Godden sometimes teased her family's Indian gardener by chanting the name of an Indian deity whose name was forbidden to be spoken out loud. This made her father angry, and he told her, "When you are in someone else's country, you will respect what they respect — and not trespass." Later, Ms. Godden became the renowned author of such children's books as *Miss Happiness and Miss Flower*.[232]

• Chian-po asked his teacher, the Buddhist priest Si-tien, why a notorious criminal was now acting with the utmost decorum after leading a life of evil. Si-tien replied, "Once these criminals have cheated, lied, and stolen enough to make themselves very wealthy, they long to be respected — and they usually can fool enough people to get what they want."[233]

Sex

• Jewish law recognizes the duty of *onah* — regular sexual intercourse between husband and wife. In fact, ancient Jewish law prescribed the minimum requirement of *onah* for couples whose husbands worked at then-common occupations — or who did no work at all. According to ancient Jewish law, people who are wealthy enough to not have to work for a living should have sexual intercourse every day; laborers should have sexual intercourse twice a week; ass-drivers, once every seven days; camel-drivers, once every 30 days; sailors, once every six months. Husbands who don't fulfill their duty of *onah* can be fined.[234]

• Jim Backus was a close friend of comedian George Burns. Once, he dropped in to see Mr. Burns while Mr. Burns was at home enjoying a cigar, a bowl of soup, and a martini. Ever the generous host, Mr. Burns offered Mr. Backus a cigar, which he declined, then he offered him a bowl of soup, which he declined, then he offered him a martini, which he declined. Finally, Mr. Burns looked up and asked, "A little sex?" (By the way, both Mr. Burns and Mr. Backus were straight. Mr. Burns was only joking.)[235]

• On TV's *Newlywed Game*, a contestant was asked, "What one thing have you mastered since you have been married?" The answer: "Sex."[236]

Spirits

• While climbing Mount Everett in the successful 1953 expedition that resulted in Edmund Hillary and Tenzing Norgay reaching the summit, the explorers sometimes passed sacred walls made of *mani* stones. On these stones was engraved a Tibetan Buddhist prayer — *Om Mani Padme Hum,* or "Hail to the Jewel of the Lotus." As part of their religion, the Sherpas walk around these walls clockwise, and in respect to the Buddhist religion, explorers such as Mr. Hillary also walk around these walls clockwise, even when the trails are narrow and dangerous. Mr. Norgay was a Buddhist, and when he reached the summit, he buried some small gifts — some candy and a pencil — for the spirit the Sherpa Buddhists believe lives on Mount Everest.[237]

• Lakshmi (LA-kshmee), the goddess of good fortune and wealth, is very active on Diwali, the Hindu Festival of Lights. That is when she visits houses and businesses. Hindus try to make Lakshmi welcome. Before Diwali, Hindus clean their house thoroughly, because if Lakshmi finds the house dirty, she will be offended. In addition, often young girls will decorate the outside of the entrances of their homes with designs and such words as "Welcome" and "Happy Diwali." When Lakshmi finds a home celebrating Diwali with lots of lights, good fellowship, and good food — often, 12 or more different kinds of sweets are served on Diwali — she blesses it.[238]

• According to the Native American tribe known as the Wampanoag, everything — including rocks and trees — has a spirit. When the Wampanoag gather a certain kind of rock to be used in a clambake, they say they are gathering the "rock people."[239]

Taoism

• According to Taoists, a very long time ago, the world was in harmony in a Golden Age. Humankind was able to communicate with the animals and the earth brought forth vegetables, fruits, and grains in abundance so that no one was hungry. Unfortunately, Humankind's Ego grew and Humankind was cut off from the rest of Nature in the Great Separation. Because of Humankind's Ego, life grew worse for Humankind. Fortunately, a few thousand years ago, people began to be born who could pass on to others what Humankind knew before the Great Separation. These "perfected spirits" were the Taoists.[240]

• A Taoist inherited a clock from his grandfather. Although the clock did not keep very good time, he valued it highly and placed it on his mantle. Unfortunately, his friends frequently made comments about the clock because it kept such poor time. Because he disliked an excessive preoccupation with time and schedules, the Taoist didn't want to get the clock fixed, so eventually he removed the hands of the clock and wrote "NOW" on its face.[241]

Television

• Here's a trivia question: What religion was John Banner, who played concentration camp guard Sergeant Schultz on the TV sitcom *Hogan's Heroes*? The correct answer is that Mr. Banner was a Jew who fled the Nazis in the late 1930s. He once said, "There is no such thing as a cuddly Nazi. I do not see Schultz as a Nazi at all: To me he represents some kind of goodness in every generation." Before his death in 1973, he wrote, "I, who am a Jew, would never be involved in anything that excuses or idealizes the German regime at that time. We are making fun of them. As proof we are shown in thirty-nine countries all over the world, except in Germany."[242]

• A 1984 TV commercial produced by the Church of Jesus Christ of Latter-Day Saints (the Mormons) showed three children engaging in a water fight. Their parents arrive, and instead of getting angry, they get a camera and start taking photographs. The genesis of the commercial occurred when the commercial's writer, Curt Dahl, saw some children engaging in a water fight — and yes, their parents arrived and started taking photos. Filming the commercial was somewhat difficult, because the little girl didn't want to get dirty. Eventually, the commercial's director, Rick Levine, bribed her with $5 to engage in the water fight.[243]

War

• During the Second World War, W.C. Fields, Lionel Barrymore, John Barrymore, and Gene Fowler were in the midst of a drinking party when they all decided to enlist, even though they were all middle-aged and suffering from one illness or another — for example, Lionel Barrymore was in a wheelchair. When they arrived at the recruiting station, a woman at the desk looked up and asked, "Who sent you? The enemy?"[244]

• During World War II, the Archbishop of Canterbury was very worried about the Cathedral at Canterbury. Prime Minister Winston Churchill assured him that everything possible had been done to keep the Cathedral safe, but the Archbishop asked, "What will happen if they score a direct hit on the Cathedral?" Churchill replied, "In that case, my dear Archbishop, you will have to regard it as a divine summons."[245]

• Humorist Ellen Orleans once brought home a new cat, and it began to fight with the old cat. Well, the two cats didn't actually fight — they just made a lot of threatening noises at each other. This gave Ms. Orleans an idea for our military policy: "Put only blanks in our nuclear warheads and Trident missiles. Make as loud a racket as you want, but no death or destruction allowed."[246]

Work

• Baizhang was a Zen master who recognized the value of manual labor. In the school of Zen he founded, everyone had to work. According to Baizhang, "Why should a monk who is sound in mind and body live like a parasite on others?" He lived to be 94 years old but kept working. When Baizhang was very old, one of his disciples became worried about him and stole his gardening tool so he could not cultivate the garden. For three days, Baizhang did not cultivate the garden, and for three days he declined to eat anything. Finally, the disciple gave him back his gardening tool. Baizhang began cultivating the garden again, and he started eating again. Baizhang's emphasis on hard work helped save Zen during a time of persecution by the Emperor Wu Zong. In 845 C.E. the Emperor issued an edict against Buddhism. Because the Zen Buddhists were self-sufficient and grew their own food, they were able to continue to flourish.[247]

• Lew Wasserman was the head of MCA, but he heard that he was about to be fired by the founder of MCA, Jules Stein. Because Mr. Stein would not fire a person who had just had a heart attack, Mr. Wasserman was able to save his job by starting a rumor that he had suffered a heart attack.[248]

• President John F. Kennedy was criticized when he gave his very young brother, Robert Kennedy, the job of Attorney General of the United States. President Kennedy replied, "I don't see what's wrong with giving Bobby a little experience before he starts to practice law."[249]

• Lifeline for the Old is a collection of programs started by Myriam Mendilow to give work and dignity to the aged in Jerusalem. At Lifeline's headquarters at Fourteen Shivtei Yisrael Street is a street sign that reads, in Hebrew, "Old Person in Path."[250]

Appendix A: Bibliography

Allen, Everett S. *Famous American Humorous Poets*. New York: Dodd, Mead & Company, 1968.

Allen, Steve. *More Funny People*. New York: Stein and Day, Publishers, 1982.

Aller, Susan Bivin. *J.M. Barrie: The Magic Behind Peter Pan*. Minneapolis, MN: Lerner Publications Company, 1994.

Alonso, Karen. Loving v. Virginia: *Interracial Marriage*. Berkeley Heights, NJ: Enslow Publications, Inc., 2000.

Atkins, Harold and Archie Newman, compilers. *Beecham Stories*. Great Britain: Futura Publications, Limited, 1978.

Banker, Stan. *Walk Cheerfully the Middleroad*. Richmond, IN: Friends United Press, 1994.

Barber, David W. *Bach, Beethoven, and the Boys*. Toronto, Canada: Sound and Vision, 1996.

Barber, David W. *If It Ain't Baroque ...: More Music History as It Ought to be Taught*. Toronto, Canada: Sound and Vision, 1992.

Benares, Camden. *Zen Without Zen Masters*. Berkeley, CA: And/Or Press, 1977.

Berger, Phil. *The Last Laugh: The World of the Stand-Up Comics*. New York: William Morris and Co., Inc., 1975.

Berra, Yogi. *"I Really Didn't Say Everything I Said."* New York: Workman Publishing Company, Inc., 1998.

Boyden, John, collector. *Stick to the Music: Scores of Orchestral Tales*. London: Souvenir Press, 1992.

Brennan, Christine. *Inside Edge: A Revealing Journey into the Secret World of Figure Skating*. New York: Scribner, 1996.

Cantor, Eddie. *As I Remember Them*. New York: Duell, Sloan and Pearce, 1963. (Mr. Cantor's collaborator for most of these pieces was Vivian M. Bowes, to whom he gives credit on the acknowledgements page.)

Cowan, Lore and Maurice. *The Wit of the Jews*. Nashville, TN: Aurora Publishers, Limited, 1970.

Cytron, Barry and Phyllis. *Myriam Mendilow: Mother of Jerusalem*. Minneapolis, MN: Lerner Publications Company, 1994.

Dole, Bob. *Great Presidential Wit*. New York: Scribner, 2001.

Dosick, Wayne. *Golden Rules: The Ten Ethical Rules Parents Need to Teach Their Children*. San Francisco, CA: HarperSanFrancisco, 1995.

Drennan, Robert E., editor. *The Algonquin Wits*. New York: The Citadel Press, 1968.

Epstein, Lawrence J. *The Haunted Smile: The Story of Jewish Comedians in America*. New York: PublicAffairs, 2001.

Farzan, Massud. *Another Way of Laughter: A Collection of Sufi Humor*. New York: E.P. Dutton & Co., Inc., 1973.

Ferguson, John, compiler and translator. *The Wit of the Greeks and Romans*. London: Leslie Frewin, 1968.

Fine, Edith Hope. *Gary Paulsen: Author and Wilderness Adventurer*. Berkeley Heights, NJ: Enslow Publications, Inc., 2000.

Ford, Corey. *The Time of Laughter*. Boston, MA: Little, Brown and Company, 1967.

Fuller, Gerald. *Stories for All Seasons*. Mystic, CT: Twenty-Third Publications, 1996.

Garagiola, Joe. *It's Anybody's Ballgame*. New York: Jove Books, 1988.

Gregory, Dick. *Nigger: An Autobiography*. With Robert Lipsyte. New York: Dutton, 1964.

Guttmacher, Peter. *Legendary Comedies*. New York: MetroBooks, 1996.

Hacohen, Rabbi Shmuel Avidor, compiler. *Touching Heaven, Touching Earth: Hassidic Humor and Wit*. Tel Aviv: Sadan Publishing, 1976.

Halliwell, Leslie. *The Filmgoer's Book of Quotes*. New Rochelle, NY: Arlington House Publishers, 1973.

Hanna, Edward; Henry Hicks; and Ted Koppel, compilers. *The Wit and Wisdom of Adlai Stevenson*. New York: Hawthorn Books, Inc., 1965.

Harris, Leon A. *The Fine Art of Political Wit*. New York: Dell Publishing Company, 1964.

Harris, Nick. *I Wish I'd Said That!* London: Octopus Books, Limited, 1984.

Haskins, Jim, and N.R. Mitgang. *Mr. Bojangles: The Story of Bill Robinson*. New York: William Morrow and Company, Inc., 1988.

Hay, Peter. *Canned Laughter*. New York: Oxford University Press, 1992.

Hecht, Ben. *Charlie: The Improbable Life and Times of Charles MacArthur*. New York: Harper & Brothers, Publishers, 1957.

Hoff, Benjamin. *The Tao of Pooh*. New York: Penguin Books, 1982.

Hoff, Benjamin. *The Te of Piglet*. New York: Penguin Books, 1992.

Holcomb, Roy K.; Samuel K. Holcomb; and Thomas K. Holcomb. *Deaf Culture Our Way: Anecdotes From the Deaf Community*. San Diego, CA: DawnSignPress, 1994.

Holland, Merlin. *The Wilde Album*. New York: Henry Holt and Company, 1997.

Huggett, Richard. *Supernatural on Stage: Ghosts and Superstitions of the Theatre*. New York: Taplinger Publishing Company, 1975.

Humphrey, Laning, compiler. *The Humor of Music and Other Oddities in the Art.* Boston, MA: Crescendo Publishing Company, 1971.

Irving, Gordon, compiler. *The Wit of the Scots.* London: Leslie Frewin Publishers, Inc., 1969.

Jessel, George. *This Way, Miss.* New York: Henry Holt and Company, 1955.

Johnson, Russell, and Steve Cox. *Here on Gilligan's Isle.* New York: HarperCollins Publishers, Inc., 1993.

Kanner, Bernice. *The 100 Best TV Commercials ... and Why They Worked.* New York: Times Books, 1999.

Karkar, Jack and Waltraud, compilers and editors. *... And They Danced On.* Wausau, WI: Aardvark Enterprises, 1989.

Klosty, James, editor and photographer. *Merce Cunningham.* New York: Saturday Review Press/E.P. Dutton and Co., Inc, 1975.

Knapp, Ron. *American Legends of Rock.* Springfield, NJ: Enslow Publications, Inc., 1996.

Kristy, Davida. *George Balanchine: American Ballet Master.* Minneapolis, MN: Lerner Publications Company, 1996.

Leonard, Sheldon. *And the Show Goes On: Broadway and Hollywood Adventures.* New York: Limelight, 1994.

Lewis, Mildred and Milton. *Famous Modern Newspaper Writers.* New York: Dodd, Mead & Company, 1962.

Linkletter, Art. *I Wish I'd Said That! My Favorite Ad-Libs of All Time.* Garden City, NY: Doubleday & Co., Inc., 1968.

Little, Jean. *Little by Little: A Writer's Education.* Ontario, Canada: Viking Kestrel, 1987.

Maccoby, Hyam, chooser and translator. *The Day God Laughed: Sayings, Fables and Entertainments of the Jewish Sages.* New York: St. Martin's Press, 1978.

Masin, Herman L. *For Laughing Out Loud: Football's Funniest Stories.* New York: Scholastic Book Services, 1954.

Massine, Léonide. *My Life in Ballet.* Edited by Phyllis Hartnoll and Robert Rubens. London: Macmillan and Co., Ltd., 1968.

Maybarduk, Linda. *The Dancer Who Flew: A Memoir of Rudolf Nureyev.* Toronto, Ontario, Canada: Tundra Books, 1999.

McCann, Sean, compiler. *The Wit of Brendan Behan.* London: Leslie Frewin Publishers, Ltd., 1968.

McCann, Sean, compiler. *The Wit of the Irish.* Nashville, TN: Aurora Publishers, Ltd., 1970.

MacMillan, Dianne M. *Diwali: Hindu Festival of Lights.* Springfield, NJ: Enslow Publications, Inc., 1997.

Matheopoulos, Helena. *The Great Tenors From Caruso to the Present*. New York: St. Martin's Press, 1999.

Miller, Claudia. *Shannon Miller: My Child, My Hero*. Norman, OK: University of Oklahoma Press, 1999.

Morgan, Henry. *Here's Morgan!* New York: Barricade Books, Inc., 1994.

Mostel, Kate, and Madeline Gilford. *170 Years of Show Business*. With Jack Gilford and Zero Mostel. New York: Random House, 1978.

Mour, Stanley I. *American Jazz Musicians*. Springfield, NJ: Enslow Publications, Inc., 1998.

Music Educators National Conference, editors. *The Gifts of Music*. Reston, VA: Music Educators National Conference, 1994.

Nachman, Gerald. *Seriously Funny: The Rebel Comedians of the 1950s and 1960s*. New York: Pantheon Books, 2003.

Naylor, Phyllis Reynolds. *How I Came to Be a Writer*. New York: Aladdin Paperbacks, 1987.

Nicholson, Frank Ernest. *Favorite Jokes of Famous People*. New York: E.P. Dutton & Co., Inc., 1928.

Nixon, Joan Lowery. *The Making of a Writer*. New York: Delacorte Press, 2002.

Oliver, Marilyn Tower. *Gay and Lesbian Rights: A Struggle*. Springfield, NJ: Enslow Publications, Inc., 1998.

Orleans, Ellen. *Can't Keep a Straight Face*. Bala Cynwyd, PA: Laugh Lines Press, 1992.

Pearson, Hesketh. *Lives of the Wits*. New York: Harper & Row, Publishers, 1962.

Perrine, Laurence. *Literature: Structure, Sound, and Sense*. 2nd ed. New York: Harcourt Brace Jovanovich, Inc., 1974.

Perry, Joel. *Funny That Way: Adventures in Fabulousness*. Los Angeles, CA: Alyson Books, 2001.

Peters, Russell M. *Clambake: A Wampanoag Tradition*. Minneapolis, MN: Lerner Publications Company, 1992.

Pike, Robert E. *Granite Laughter and Marble Tears*. Brattleboro, VT: Stephen Daye Press, 1938.

Podgórecki, Adam. *The Tales of Si-tien*. London: Poets' and Painters' Press, 1973.

Poley, Irvin C., and Ruth Verlenden Poley. *Friendly Anecdotes*. New York: Harper & Brothers, Publishers, 1950.

Pratt, Paula Bryant. *Martha Graham*. San Diego, CA: Lucent Books, 1995.

Primack, Ben, adapter and editor. *The Ben Hecht Show: Impolitic Observations from the Freest Thinker of 1950s Television*. Jefferson, NC: McFarland & Company, Inc., Publishers, 1993.

Procter-Gregg, Humphrey. *Beecham Remembered*. London: Gerald Duckworth & Company, Limited, 1976.

Rabinowicz, Rabbi Dr. H. *A Guide to Hassidism*. New York: Thomas Yoseloff, 1960.

Richie, Donald. *Zen Inklings*. New York: John Weatherhill, Inc., 1982.

Roessel, Monty. *Kinaaldá: A Navajo Girl Grows Up*. Minneapolis, MN: Lerner Publications Company, 1993.

Rogers, Fred. *The World According to Mister Rogers*. New York: Hyperion, 2003.

Rosten, Leo. *People I Have Loved, Known or Admired*. New York: McGraw-Hill Book Company, 1970.

Russell, Anna. *I'm Not Making This Up, You Know: The Autobiography of the Queen of Musical Parody*. New York: The Continuum Publishing Company, 1985.

Samra, Cal and Rose, editors. *More Holy Hilarity*. Colorado Springs, CO: WaterBrook Press, 1999.

Samra, Cal and Rose, editors. *More Holy Humor*. Colorado Springs, CO: WaterBrook Press, 1997.

Schafer, Kermit. *All Time Great Bloopers*. New York: Avenel Books, 1973.

Schafer, Kermit. *Best of Bloopers*. New York: Avenel Books, 1973.

Schraff, Anne. *Coretta Scott King: Striving for Civil Rights*. Springfield, NJ: Enslow Publications, Inc., 1997.

Silverman, Stephen M. *Funny Ladies: The Women Who Make Us Laugh*. New York: Harry N. Abrams, Inc., 1999.

Skipper, John C. *Umpires: Classic Baseball Stories from the Men Who Made the Calls*. Jefferson, NC, and London: McFarland and Company, Inc., Publishers, 1997.

Slezak, Walter. *What Time's the Next Swan?* Garden City, NY: Doubleday and Co., Inc., 1962.

Slide, Anthony. *Eccentrics of Comedy*. Lanham, MD, and London: The Scarecrow Press, Inc., 1998.

Smaridge, Norah. *Famous Modern Storytellers for Young People*. New York: Dodd, Mead & Company, 1969.

Smith, Bob. *Openly Bob*. New York: William Morrow and Company, Inc., 1997.

Smith, H. Allen. *Buskin' With H. Allen Smith*. New York: Trident Press, 1968.

Smith, H. Allen. *To Hell in a Handbasket*. Garden City, NY: Doubleday & Company, Inc., 1962.

Smith, O. *Recollections of O. Smith, Comedian*. New York: Theatre Library Association, 1979.

Smith, Ron. *Comic Support*. New York: Carol Publishing Group, 1993.

Sorensen, Jeff. *Bob Newhart*. New York: St. Martin's Press, 1988.

Spies, Karen Bornemann. *Franklin Delano Roosevelt*. Springfield, NJ: Enslow Publications, Inc., 1999.

Stevens, William Oliver. *Famous Humanitarians*. New York: Dodd, Mead & Company, 1953.

Stewart, Whitney. *Sir Edmund Hillary: To Everest and Beyond*. Minneapolis, MN: Lerner Publications Company, 1996.

Surge, Frank. *Singers of the Blues*. Minneapolis, MN: Lerner Publications Company, 1969.

Svoboda, Melannie. *Everyday Epiphanies*. Mystic, CT: Twenty-Third Publications, 1997.

Sykes, Adam, and Iain Sproat, compilers. *The Wit of Westminster*. London: Leslie Frewin, Limited, 1967.

Taylor, Robert Lewis. *W.C. Fields: His Follies and Fortunes*. Garden City, NY: Doubleday and Company, Inc., 1949.

Telushkin, Rabbi Joseph. *Jewish Wisdom: Ethical, Spiritual, and Historical Lessons from the Great Works and Thinkers*. New York: William Morrow and Company, Inc., 1994.

Terry, Walter. *Ted Shawn: Father of American Dance*. New York: The Dial Press, 1976.

Thomas, Bob. *Bud & Lou: The Abbott and Costello Story*. Philadelphia, PA: J.B. Lippincott Company, 1977.

Treston, Kevin. *Five Dynamic Dimensions for Effective Teaching*. Mystic, CT: Twenty-Third Publications, 1997.

Troy, Con. *Laugh with Hugh Troy, World's Greatest Practical Joker*. Wyomissing, PA: Trojan Books, 1983.

True, Cynthia. *American Scream: The Bill Hicks Story*. New York: HarperEntertainment, 2002.

Tsai, Chih-Chung (editor and illustrator) and Kok Kok Kiang (translator). *Origins of Zen*. Singapore: Asiapac, 1990.

Twain, Mark. *Life on the Mississippi*. New York: Oxford University Press, 1996.

Unterbrink, Mary. *Funny Women: American Comediennes, 1860-1985*. Jefferson, NC: McFarland and Co., Inc., Publishers, 1987.

Wade, Don. *"And Then Arnie Told Chi Chi ...."* Chicago, IL: Contemporary Books, 1993.

Wagenknecht, Edward. *Seven Daughters of the Theater*. Norman, OK: University of Oklahoma Press, 1964.

Wagner, Alan. *Prima Donnas and Other Wild Beasts*. Larchmont, NY: Argonaut Books, 1961.

Warren, Roz, editor. *Revolutionary Laughter: The World of Women Comics.* Freedom, CA: The Crossing Press, 1995.

Weatherby, W.J. *Jackie Gleason: An Intimate Portrait.* New York: Berkley Books, 1992.

Wilde, Larry. *The Great Comedians.* Secaucus, NJ: The Citadel Press, 1968.

Wilde, Larry. *How the Great Comedy Writers Create Laughter.* Chicago, IL: Nelson-Hall, Inc., 1976.

Williams, John A., and Dennis A. Williams. *If I Stop I'll Die: The Comedy and Tragedy of Richard Pryor.* New York: Thunder's Mouth Press, 1991.

Wilner, Barry. *Michelle Kwan: Star Figure Skater.* Berkeley Heights, NJ: Enslow Publications, Inc., 2001.

Wilner, Barry. *Tara Lipinski: Star Figure Skater.* Berkeley Heights, NJ: Enslow Publications, Inc., 2001.

Wilson, Craig McNair. *YHWH is Not a Radio Station in Minneapolis.* San Francisco, CA: Harper and Row, Publishers, 1983.

Woolf, Vicki. *Dancing in the Vortex: The Story of Ida Rubinstein.* Australia: Harwood Academic Publishers, 2000.

Woollcott, Alexander. *Enchanted Aisles.* New York: G.P. Putnam's Sons, 1924.

Worland, Bill. *"Fumble Four Bars In."* London: Minerva Press, 1996.

Yamane, Linda. *Weaving a California Tradition: A Native American Basketmaker.* Minneapolis, MN: Lerner Publications Company, 1997.

Youngman, Henny. *Take My Life, Please!* With Neal Karlen. New York: William Morris and Company, Inc., 1991.

Zimmerman, Paul D., and Burt Goldblatt. *The Marx Brothers at the Movies.* New York: G.P. Putnam's Sons, 1968.

Appendix B: About the Author

It was a dark and stormy night. Suddenly a cry rang out, and on a hot summer night in 1954, Josephine, wife of Carl Bruce, gave birth to a boy — me. Unfortunately, this young married couple allowed Reuben Saturday, Josephine's brother, to name their first-born. Reuben, aka "The Joker," decided that Bruce was a nice name, so he decided to name me Bruce Bruce. I have gone by my middle name — David — ever since.

Being named Bruce David Bruce hasn't been all bad. Bank tellers remember me very quickly, so I don't often have to show an ID. It can be fun in charades, also. When I was a counselor as a teenager at Camp Echoing Hills in Warsaw, Ohio, a fellow counselor gave the signs for "sounds like" and "two words," then she pointed to a bruise on her leg twice. Bruise Bruise? Oh yeah, Bruce Bruce is the answer!

Uncle Reuben, by the way, gave me a haircut when I was in kindergarten. He cut my hair short and shaved a small bald spot on the back of my head. My mother wouldn't let me go to school until the bald spot grew out again.

Of all my brothers and sisters (six in all), I am the only transplant to Athens, Ohio. I was born in Newark, Ohio, and have lived all around Southeastern Ohio. However, I moved to Athens to go to Ohio University and have never left.

At Ohio U, I never could make up my mind whether to major in English or Philosophy, so I got a bachelor's degree with a double major in both areas, then I added a Master of Arts degree in English and a Master of Arts degree in Philosophy. Yes, I have my MAMA degree.

Currently, and for a long time to come (I eat fruits and veggies), I am spending my retirement writing books such as *Nadia Comaneci: Perfect 10*, *The Funniest People in Comedy*, *Homer's* Iliad: *A Retelling in Prose*, and *William Shakespeare's* Hamlet: *A Retelling in Prose*.

If all goes well, I will publish one or two books a year for the rest of my life. (On the other hand, a good way to make God laugh is to tell Her your plans.)

By the way, my sister Brenda Kennedy writes romances such as *A New Beginning* and *Shattered Dreams*.

Appendix C: Some Books by David Bruce

Anecdote Collections

250 Anecdotes About Opera

250 Anecdotes About Religion

250 Anecdotes About Religion: Volume 2

250 Music Anecdotes

Be a Work of Art: 250 Anecdotes and Stories

The Coolest People in Art: 250 Anecdotes

The Coolest People in the Arts: 250 Anecdotes

The Coolest People in Books: 250 Anecdotes

The Coolest People in Comedy: 250 Anecdotes

Create, Then Take a Break: 250 Anecdotes

Don't Fear the Reaper: 250 Anecdotes

The Funniest People in Art: 250 Anecdotes

The Funniest People in Books: 250 Anecdotes

The Funniest People in Books, Volume 2: 250 Anecdotes

The Funniest People in Books, Volume 3: 250 Anecdotes

The Funniest People in Comedy: 250 Anecdotes

The Funniest People in Dance: 250 Anecdotes

The Funniest People in Families: 250 Anecdotes

The Funniest People in Families, Volume 2: 250 Anecdotes

The Funniest People in Families, Volume 3: 250 Anecdotes

The Funniest People in Families, Volume 4: 250 Anecdotes

The Funniest People in Families, Volume 5: 250 Anecdotes

The Funniest People in Families, Volume 6: 250 Anecdotes

The Funniest People in Movies: 250 Anecdotes

The Funniest People in Music: 250 Anecdotes

The Funniest People in Music, Volume 2: 250 Anecdotes

The Funniest People in Music, Volume 3: 250 Anecdotes

The Funniest People in Neighborhoods: 250 Anecdotes

The Funniest People in Relationships: 250 Anecdotes

The Funniest People in Sports: 250 Anecdotes

The Funniest People in Sports, Volume 2: 250 Anecdotes

The Funniest People in Television and Radio: 250 Anecdotes

The Funniest People in Theater: 250 Anecdotes

The Funniest People Who Live Life: 250 Anecdotes
The Funniest People Who Live Life, Volume 2: 250 Anecdotes
The Kindest People Who Do Good Deeds, Volume 1: 250 Anecdotes
The Kindest People Who Do Good Deeds, Volume 2: 250 Anecdotes
Maximum Cool: 250 Anecdotes
The Most Interesting People in Movies: 250 Anecdotes
The Most Interesting People in Politics and History: 250 Anecdotes
The Most Interesting People in Politics and History, Volume 2: 250 Anecdotes
The Most Interesting People in Politics and History, Volume 3: 250 Anecdotes
The Most Interesting People in Religion: 250 Anecdotes
The Most Interesting People in Sports: 250 Anecdotes
The Most Interesting People Who Live Life: 250 Anecdotes
The Most Interesting People Who Live Life, Volume 2: 250 Anecdotes
Reality is Fabulous: 250 Anecdotes and Stories
Resist Psychic Death: 250 Anecdotes
Seize the Day: 250 Anecdotes and Stories

[1]Source: O. Smith, *Recollections of O. Smith, Comedian*, pp. 22-23.

[2]Source: Peter Guttmacher, *Legendary Comedies*, p. 69.

[3]Source: Bob Smith, *Openly Bob*, p. 74.

[4]Source: Richard Huggett, *Supernatural on Stage*, p. 37.

[5]Source: Sam Snead, *The Game I Love*, p. 90.

[6]Source: Peter Hay, *Canned Laughter*, p. 208.

[7]Source: Bernice Kanner, *The 100 Best TV Commercials*, p. 164.

[8]Source: Leo Rosten, *People I Have Loved, Known or Admired*, p. 17.

[9]Source: H. Allen Smith, *Buskin' With H. Allen Smith*, p. 202.

[10]Source: William H. Sessions, collector, *Laughter in Quaker Grey*, p. 118.

[11]Source: Ron Smith, *Comic Support*, p. 179.

[12]Source: Sean McCann, compiler, *The Wit of the Irish*, p. 80.

[13]Source: Gerald Fuller, *Stories for All Seasons*, pp. 102-3.

[14]Source: Hyam Maccoby, chooser and translator, *The Day God Laughed*, p. 140.

[15]Source: Anna Russell, *I'm Not Making This Up, You Know*, p. 21.

[16]Source: John C. Skipper, *Umpires*, p. 70.

[17]Source: Art Linkletter, *I Wish I'd Said That!*, p. 28.

[18]Source: Stan Banker, *Walk Cheerfully the Middleroad*, pp. 111-112.

[19]Source: Camden Benares, *Zen Without Zen Masters*, p. 32.

[20]Source: Sean McCann, compiler, *The Wit of Brendan Behan*, pp. 9, 72.

[21]Source: Hesketh Pearson, *Lives of the Wits*, pp. 199-200.

[22]Source: Mildred and Milton Lewis, *Famous Modern Newspaper Writers*, p. 92.

[23]Source: Barry and Phyllis Cytron, *Myriam Mendilow: Mother of Jerusalem*, pp. 21-23.

[24]Source: Mildred and Milton Lewis, *Famous Modern Newspaper Writers*, pp. 40-41.

[25]Source: Jeff Sorensen, *Bob Newhart*, p. 41.

[26]Source: Bob Thomas, *Bud & Lou*, p. 151.

[27]Source: Chapter 3 of Robert Lewis Taylor, *W.C. Fields: His Follies and Fortunes*.

[28]Source: Larry Wilde, *How the Great Comedy Writers Create Laughter*, p. 24.

[29]Source: Steve Allen, *More Funny People*, p. 302.

[30]Source: Bob Thomas, *Bud & Lou*, pp. 124-125.

[31]Source: Arthur Marx, *Life With Groucho*, pp. 58-60.

[32]Source: Sheldon Leonard, *And the Show Goes On*, pp. 104-105.

[33]Source: Roz Warren, editor, *Revolutionary Laughter*, pp. 62-63.

[34]Source: Stephen M. Silverman, *Funny Ladies*, p. 89.

[35]Source: Vicki Woolf, *Dancing in the Vortex: The Story of Ida Rubinstein*, p. 33.

[36]Source: Dick Gregory, *Nigger*, pp. 46, 48.

[37]Source: Mary Unterbrink, *Funny Women*, p. 84.

[38]Source: Susan Bivin Aller, *J.M. Barrie: The Magic Behind Peter Pan*, pp. 114-115.

[39]Source: Adam Podgórecki, *The Tales of Si-tien*, pp. 25-26.

[40]Source: Dianne M. MacMillan, *Diwali: Hindu Festival of Lights*, pp. 4-5, 34, 40.

[41]Source: Eddie Cantor, *As I Remember Them*, pp. 37-38.

[42]Source: Claudia Miller, *Shannon Miller: My Child, My Hero*, p. 66.

[43]Source: Edith Hope Fine, *Gary Paulsen: Author and Wilderness Adventurer*, pp. 13-14.

[44]Source: Walter Slezak, *What Time's the Next Swan?*, p. 208.

[45]Source: Everett S. Allen, *Famous American Humorous Poets*, p. 52.

[46]Source: Alan Wagner, *Prima Donnas and Other Wild Beasts*, pp. 139-140.

[47]Source: Bill Worland, *"Fumble Four Bars In"*, p. 93.

[48]Source: Music Educators National Conference, editors, *The Gifts of Music*, p. 182.

[49]Source: Barry Wilner, *Michelle Kwan: Star Figure Skater*, p. 18.

[50]Source: Kermit Schafer, *Best of Bloopers*, p. 42.

[51]Source: Barry Wilner, *Tara Lipinski: Star Figure Skater*, p. 12.

[52]Source: Steve Allen, *More Funny People*, p. 91.

[53]Source: Jack and Waltraud Karkar, compilers and editors, *... And They Danced On*, p. 48.

[54]Source: Cal and Rose Samra, *More Holy Hilarity*, pp. 8, 10.

[55]Source: Fred Rogers, *The World According to Mister Rogers*, pp. 126-127.

[56]Source: Russell Johnson and Steve Cox, *Here on Gilligan's Isle*, pp. 174-175.

[57]Source: Jim Haskins and N.R. Mitgang, *Mr. Bojangles*, p. 295.

[58]Source: John Ferguson, compiler and translator, *The Wit of the Greeks and Romans*, p. 18.

[59]Source: Henry Morgan, *Here's Morgan!*, p. 179.

[60]Source: John A. Williams and Dennis A. Williams, *If I Stop I'll Die*, p. 22.

[61]Source: Sean McCann, compiler, *The Wit of the Irish*, p. 77.

[62]Source: Ron Knapp, *American Legends of Rock*, pp. 17-18.

[63]Source: Ben Hecht, *Charlie: The Improbable Life and Times of Charles MacArthur*, pp. 36-37.

[64]Source: Phyllis Reynolds Naylor, *How I Came to Be a Writer*, p. 131.

[65]Source: Corey Ford, *The Time of Laughter*, p. 21.

[66]Source: Henri Fesquet, collector, *Wit and Wisdom of Good Pope John*, p. 91.

[67]Source: Melannie Svoboda, *Everyday Epiphanies*, p. 115.

[68]Source: Marilyn Tower Oliver, *Gay and Lesbian Rights: A Struggle*, pp. 48-49.

[69]Source: Leslie Halliwell, *The Filmgoer's Book of Quotes*, p. 186.

[70]Source: Walter Terry, *Ted Shawn: Father of American Dance*, pp. 31-32. The New American Standard Bible translates Psalm 150:4 as "Praise Him with timbrel and dancing; Praise Him with stringed instruments and pipe."

[71]Source: Paula Bryant Pratt, *Martha Graham*, pp. 86-87.

[72]Source: Léonide Massine, *My Life in Ballet*, p. 62.

[73]Source: Davida Kristy, *George Balanchine: American Ballet Master*, p. 121.

[74]Source: Linda Maybarduk, *The Dancer Who Flew*, p. 25.

[75]Source: Paula Bryant Pratt, *Martha Graham*, p. 18.

[76]Source: Léonide Massine, *My Life in Ballet*, p. 242.

[77]Source: W.J. Weatherby, *Jackie Gleason: An Intimate Portrait*, pp. 168, 190.

[78]Source: Robert E. Pike, *Granite Laughter and Marble Tears*, pp. 32-33.

[79]Source: Nick Harris, *I Wish I'd Said That!*, pp. 84, 106.

[80]Source: Joan Lowery Nixon, *The Making of a Writer*, pp. 51-52.

[81]Source: Hesketh Pearson, *Lives of the Wits*, pp. 166, 177.

^[82]Source: Merlin Holland, *The Wilde Album*, pp. 55, 184.

[82]Source: Merlin Holland, *The Wilde Album*, pp. 55, 184.

[83]Source: Kate Mostel and Madeline Gilford, *170 Years of Show Business*, pp. 131-132.

[84]Source: W.J. Weatherby, *Jackie Gleason: An Intimate Portrait*, pp. 135, 150.

[85]Source: Robert E. Drennan, ed., *The Algonquin Wits*, pp. 79, 92.

[86]Source: Anthony Slide, *Eccentrics of Comedy*, p. 43.

[87]Source: Richard Huggett, *Supernatural on Stage*, pp. 96-97.

[88]Source: Robert E. Pike, *Granite Laughter and Marble Tears*, p, 14.

[89]Source: Ben Primack, adapter and editor, *The Ben Hecht Show*, p. 184.

[90]Source: Eddie Cantor, *As I Remember Them*, p. 85.

[91]Source: Leo Rosten, *People I Have Loved, Known or Admired*, p. 31.

[92]Source: Art Linkletter, *I Wish I'd Said That!*, p. 118.

[93]Source: Mark Twain's *Life on the Mississippi*, Oxford Mark Twain, p. 441.

[94]Source: George Jessel, *This Way, Miss*, p. 228.

[95]Source: John C. Skipper, *Umpires*, pp. 130, 133.

[96]Source: Henry Morgan, *Here's Morgan!*, p. 262.

[97] Source: Garrison Keillor, "Skip the Big Belch with Gay Paree visit." *Chicago Tribune*. 31 December 2008 <http://www.chicagotribune.com/news/columnists/chi-oped1231keillordec31,0,4812040.column>.

[98]Source: Jean Little, *Little by Little: A Writer's Education*, p. 201.

[99]Source: Rabbi Dr. H. Rabinowicz, *A Guide to Hassidism*, p. 76.

[100] Source: "'If you could kiss anyone in the world, who would it be?': Francesca Gallio, 11, interviews Simon Cowell." *The Guardian*. 31 January 2009 <http://www.guardian.co.uk/lifeandstyle/2009/jan/31/simon-cowell-interview>.

[101]Source: Wayne Dosick, *Golden Rules*, p. 120.

[102]Source: Rabbi Joseph Telushkin, *Jewish Wisdom*, p. 201.

[103]Source: Merlin Holland, *The Wilde Album*, p. 128.

[104]Source: Roz Warren, editor, *Revolutionary Laughter*, p. 80.

[105]Source: Kevin Treston, *Five Dynamic Dimensions for Effective Teaching*, p. 14.

[106] Source: Cal and Rose Samra, editors, *More Holy Humor*, p. 37.

[107] Source: Cynthia True, *American Scream: The Bill Hicks Story*, p. 24.

[108] Source: John Ferguson, compiler and translator, *The Wit of the Greeks and Romans*, p. 12.

[109] Source: Phil Berger, *The Last Laugh*, p. 41.

[110] Source: Davida Kristy, *George Balanchine: American Ballet Master*, pp. 18, 26.

[111] Source: Massud Farzan, *Another Way of Laughter*, p. 28.

[112] Source: Anthony Slide, *Eccentrics of Comedy*, p. 127.

[113] Source: Bob Smith, *Openly Bob*, p. 40.

[114] Source: Stanley I. Mour, *American Jazz Musicians*, p. 31.

[115] Source: Larry Wilde, *The Great Comedians*, p. 223.

[116] Source: Phyllis Reynolds Naylor, *How I Came to Be a Writer*, p. 123.

[117] Source: Stan Banker, *Walk Cheerfully the Middleroad*, p. 139.

[118] Source: Stephen M. Silverman, *Funny Ladies*, p. 34.

[119] Source: Yogi Berra, *"I Really Didn't Say Everything I Said,"* p. 80.

[120] Source: Claudia Miller, *Shannon Miller: My Child, My Hero*, pp. 118-119.

[121] Source: Ben Hecht, *Charlie: The Improbable Life and Times of Charles MacArthur*, p. 135.

[122] Source: Sean McCann, compiler, *The Wit of Brendan Behan*, p. 34.

[123] Source: Rabbi Dr. H. Rabinowicz, *A Guide to Hassidism*, p. 99.

[124] Source: Gordon Irving, compiler, *The Wit of the Scots*, p. 42.

[125] Source: Gerald Nachman, *Seriously Funny*, pp. 62, 85.

[126] Source: Don Wade, *"And Then Arnie Told Chi Chi...,"* p. 172.

[127] Source: Rabbi Shmuel Avidor Hacohen, compiler, *Touching Heaven, Touching Earth: Hassidic Humor and Wit*, p. 131.

[128] Source: Lore and Maurice Cowan, *The Wit of the Jews*, p. 139.

[129] Source: Edward Hanna, Henry Hicks, and Ted Koppel, compilers, *The Wit and Wisdom of Adlai Stevenson*, p. 69.

[130] Source: Phil Berger, *The Last Laugh*, p. 277.

[131] Source: Susan Bivin Aller, *J.M. Barrie: The Magic Behind Peter Pan*, pp. 95-96, 104.

[132] Source: Humphrey Procter-Gregg, *Beecham Remembered*, p. 4.

[133] Source: Jim Haskins and N.R. Mitgang, *Mr. Bojangles*, p. 291.

[134] Source: H. Allen Smith, *To Hell in a Handbasket*, pp. 62-63.

[135] Source: Laning Humphrey, compiler, *The Humor of Music and Other Oddities in the Art*, pp. 89-90.

[136] Source: Kermit Schafer, *All Time Great Bloopers*, p. 86.

[137] Source: Cal and Rose Samra, *More Holy Hilarity*, pp. 97-100.

[138] Source: Bob Dole, *Great Presidential Wit*, p. 93.

[139] Source: John Boyden, collector, *Stick to the Music: Scores of Orchestral Tales*, pp. 41-42.

[140] Source: Whitney Stewart, *Sir Edmund Hillary: To Everest and Beyond*, p. 57.

[141] Source: Joan Lowery Nixon, *The Making of a Writer*, pp. 73-76.

[142] Source: Joe Garagiola, *It's Anybody's Ballgame*, pp. 99-101.

[143] Source: Karen Bornemann Spies, *Franklin Delano Roosevelt*, p. 14.

[144] Source: Sam Snead, *The Game I Love*, p. 126.

[145] Source: H. Allen Smith, *Buskin' With H. Allen Smith*, p. 85.

[146] Source: Susan Edwards, *Erma Bombeck*, pp. 53-54.

[147] Source: Karen Alonso, Loving v. Virginia: *Interracial Marriage*, p. 67.

[148] Source: Gordon Irving, compiler, *The Wit of the Scots*, p. 74.

[149] Source: Nick Harris, *I Wish I'd Said That!*, p. 57.

[150] Source: Christine Brennan, *Inside Edge*, p. 73.

[151] Source: Larry Wilde, *How the Great Comedy Writers Create Laughter*, p. 25.

[152] Source: Roy. K. Holcomb, Samuel K. Holcomb, and Thomas K. Holcomb, *Deaf Culture Our Way*, p. 9.

[153] Source: Frank Ernest Nicholson, *Favorite Jokes of Famous People*, pp. 195-196.

[154] Source: Jeff Sorensen, *Bob Newhart*, pp. 127-128.

[155] Source: James Klosty, editor and photographer, *Merce Cunningham*, p. 57.

[156] Source: Kermit Schafer, *Best of Bloopers*, p. 100.

[157] Source: Rabbi Shmuel Avidor Hacohen, compiler, *Touching Heaven, Touching Earth: Hassidic Humor and Wit*, p. 118.

[158] Source: Henny Youngman, *Take My Life, Please!*, p. 128.

[159]Source: Lawrence J. Epstein, *The Haunted Smile*, pp. 173-174.

[160]Source: Cynthia True, *American Scream: The Bill Hicks Story*, p. 103.

[161]Source: Peter Guttmacher, *Legendary Comedies*, p. 43, 45.

[162]Source: Robert E. Drennan, ed., *The Algonquin Wits*, p. 154.

[163]Source: Leslie Halliwell, *The Filmgoer's Book of Quotes*, p. 122.

[164]Source: Ron Knapp, *American Legends of Rock*, pp. 101-102.

[165]Source: Walter Slezak, *What Time's the Next Swan?*, pp. 73-74.

[166]Source: Frank Surge, *Singers of the Blues*, pp. 35, 49.

[167]Source: Larry Wilde, *The Great Comedians*, p. 144.

[168]Source: Edward Wagenknecht, *Seven Daughters of the Theater*, p. 160.

[169] Source: David W. Barber, *If It Ain't Baroque...*, p. 46.

[170]Source: David W. Barber, *Bach, Beethoven, and the Boys*, p. 80.

[171]Source: Laning Humphrey, compiler, *The Humor of Music and Other Oddities in the Art*, pp. 10-11.

[172]Source: Harold Atkins and Archie Newman, *Beecham Stories*, p. 56.

[173]Source: John Boyden, collector, *Stick to the Music: Scores of Orchestral Tales*, p. 27.

[174]Source: Yogi Berra, *"I Really Didn't Say Everything I Said,"* p. 79.

[175]Source: David W. Barber, *If It Ain't Baroque...*, p. 47.

[176]Source: William Oliver Stevens, *Famous Humanitarians*, pp. 97-100.

[177]Source: Corey Ford, *The Time of Laughter*, pp. 52, 54.

[178]Source: Karen Bornemann Spies, *Franklin Delano Roosevelt*, pp. 27-28, 33-34.

[179]Source: Paul D. Zimmerman and Burt Goldblatt, *The Marx Brothers at the Movies*, pp. 83, 224.

[180]Source: Stanley I. Mour, *American Jazz Musicians*, pp. 40, 42, 44.

[181]Source: David W. Barber, *Bach, Beethoven, and the Boys*, pp. 70-71.

[182]Source: Craig McNair Wilson, *YHWH is Not a Radio Station in Minneapolis*, p. 15.

[183]Source: a Lifetime *Intimate Portrait* program featuring Mother Teresa.

[184]Source: Mary Unterbrink, *Funny Women*, p. 93.

[185]Source: a Lifetime *Intimate Portrait* program featuring Mother Teresa.

[186]Source: George Jessel, *This Way, Miss*, pp. 182-3.

[187]Source: Roy K. Holcomb, Samuel K. Holcomb, and Thomas K. Holcomb, *Deaf Culture Our Way*, p. 76.

[188]Source: Con Troy, *Laugh with Hugh Troy*, pp. 16-19.

[189]Source: Anna Russell, *I'm Not Making This Up, You Know*, p. 94.

[190]Source: Jack and Waltraud Karkar, compilers and editors, *... And They Danced On*, p. 138.

[191]Source: Ben Primack, adapter and editor, *The Ben Hecht Show*, p. 133.

[192]Source: Irvin C. Poley and Ruth Verlenden Poley, *Friendly Anecdotes*, p. 24.

[193]Source: Richard Huggett, *Supernatural on Stage*, p. 20.

[194]Source: Joel Perry, *Funny That Way: Adventures in Fabulousness*, p. 10.

[195]Source: Joe Garagiola, *It's Anybody's Ballgame*, pp. 95-96.

[196]Source: Gerald Fuller, *Stories for All Seasons*, p. 79.

[197]Source: Linda Maybarduk, *The Dancer Who Flew*, p. 20.

[198]Source: Fred Rogers, *The World According to Mister Rogers*, pp. 66-67.

[199]Source: Linda Yamane, *Weaving a California Tradition: A Native American Basketmaker*, p. 29.

[200]Source: Monty Roessel, *Kinaaldá: A Navajo Girl Grows Up*, p. 38.

[201]Source: Harold Atkins and Archie Newman, *Beecham Stories*, p. 30.

[202]Source: Edward Hanna, Henry Hicks, and Ted Koppel, compilers, *The Wit and Wisdom of Adlai Stevenson*, p. 78.

[203]Source: Anne Schraff, *Coretta Scott King: Striving for Civil Rights*, p. 51.

[204]Source: Bob Dole, *Great Presidential Wit*, p. 127.

[205]Source: Rabbi Joseph Telushkin, *Jewish Wisdom*, p. 499.

[206]Source: Lawrence J. Epstein, *The Haunted Smile*, p. 124.

[207]Source: Christine Brennan, *Inside Edge*, p. 61.

[208]Source: Peter Hay, *Canned Laughter*, p. 158.

[209]Source: Joel Perry, *Funny That Way: Adventures in Fabulousness*, p. 97.

[210]Source: Frank Surge, *Singers of the Blues*, p. 35.

[211]Source: Sheldon Leonard, *And the Show Goes On*, pp. 80-81.

[212]Source: Leon A. Harris, *The Fine Art of Political Wit*, p. 46.

[213]Source: Lore and Maurice Cowan, *The Wit of the Jews*, p. 141.

[214]Source: Donald Richie, *Zen Inklings*, pp. 23-24.

[215]Source: Massud Farzan, *Another Way of Laughter*, p. 1.

[216]Source: Con Troy, *Laugh with Hugh Troy*, pp. 43-44.

[217]Source: Ellen Orleans, *Can't Keep a Straight Face*, p. 21.

[218]Source: Gerald Nachman, *Seriously Funny*, p. 597.

[219]Source: Adam Sykes and Iain Sproat, compilers, *The Wit of Westminster*, p. 92.

[220]Source: William Oliver Stevens, *Famous Humanitarians*, p. 114.

[221]Source: Humphrey Procter-Gregg, *Beecham Remembered*, p. 66.

[222]Source: Benjamin Hoff, *The Te of Piglet*, pp. 156-157.

[223]Source: Marilyn Tower Oliver, *Gay and Lesbian Rights: A Struggle*, p. 29.

[224]Source: Frank Ernest Nicholson, *Favorite Jokes of Famous People*, p. 15.

[225]Source: Groucho Marx, *Groucho and Me*, p. 322.

[226]Source: Herman L. Masin, *For Laughing Out Loud: Football's Funniest Stories*, pp. 38-39.

[227]Source: Irvin C. Poley and Ruth Verlenden Poley, *Friendly Anecdotes*, pp. 70-71.

[228]Source: Herman L. Masin, *For Laughing Out Loud: Football's Funniest Stories*, pp. 25-26.

[229]Source: Laurence Perrine, *Literature: Structure, Sound, and Sense*, p. 675.

[230]Source: Alexander Woollcott, *Enchanted Aisles*, pp. 235-236.

[231]Source: *Acts*, chapter 20.

[232]Source: Norah Smaridge, *Famous Modern Storytellers for Young People*, pp. 68-69.

[233]Source: Adam Podgórecki, *The Tales of Si-tien*, p. 30.

[234]Source: Hyam Maccoby, chooser and translator, *The Day God Laughed*, pp. 79, 81.

[235]Source: Russell Johnson and Steve Cox, *Here on Gilligan's Isle*, p. 48.

[236]Source: Kermit Schafer, *All Time Great Bloopers*, p. 16.

[237]Source: Whitney Stewart, *Sir Edmund Hillary: To Everest and Beyond*, pp. 9-10, 41.

[238]Source: Dianne M. MacMillan, *Diwali: Hindu Festival of Lights*, pp. 22-23, 25-26, 29-30.

[239]Source: Russell M. Peters, *Clambake: A Wampanoag Tradition*, p. 14.

[240]Source: Benjamin Hoff, *The Te of Piglet*, pp. 13-16.

[241]Source: Camden Benares, *Zen Without Zen Masters*, p. 87.

[242]Source: Ron Smith, *Comic Support*, pp. 18-19.

[243]Source: Bernice Kanner, *The 100 Best TV Commercials*, pp. 197-198.

[244]Source: Robert Lewis Taylor, *W.C. Fields: His Follies and Fortunes*, pp. 264-265.

[245]Source: Adam Sykes and Iain Sproat, compilers, *The Wit of Westminster*, pp. 49-50.

[246]Source: Ellen Orleans, *Can't Keep a Straight Face*, p. 30.

[247]Source: Tsai Chih Chung (editor and illustrator) and Kok Kok Kiang (translator), *Origins of Zen*, pp. 62, 64-65.

[248]Source: Henny Youngman, *Take My Life, Please!*, p. 174.

[249]Source: Leon A. Harris, *The Fine Art of Political Wit*, p. 260.

[250]Source: Barry and Phyllis Cytron, *Myriam Mendilow: Mother of Jerusalem*, pp. 10-11.